DIRTY
FRENCH

DIRTY FRENCH

EVERYDAY SLANG FROM
"WHAT'S UP?" TO "F*%# OFF!"

•••••Adrien Clautrier and Henry Rowe

Illustrated by Lindsay Mack

Ulysses Press

Published by:
Ulysses Press
P.O. Box 3440
Berkeley, CA 94703
www.ulyssespress.com

ISBN10: 1-56975-658-9
ISBN13: 978-1-56975-658-4
Library of Congress Control Number: 2007907739

Printed in Canada by Webcom

10 9 8 7 6 5 4

Acquisitions Editor: Nick Denton-Brown
Managing Editor: Claire Chun
Copyeditors: Mark Rhynsburger, Mark Woodworth
Proofreader: Lauren Harrison
Production: Tamara Kowalski
Interior Design: what!design @ whatweb.com
Cover Design: Double R Design
Back Cover Illustration: Lindsay Mack

Distributed by Publishers Group West

This book is dedicated to Eric and to the soccer club ASPEN/St. Cloud

TABLE OF CONTENTS

Using this Book   **1**

[1]   Howdy French   **4**

[2]   Friendly French   **18**

[3]   Party French   **31**

[4]   Body French   **47**

[5]   Horny French   **58**

[6]   Angry French   **80**

[7]   Poppy French   **93**

[8]   Sporty French   **110**

[9]   Hungry French   **121**

About the Authors   **136**

USING
THIS BOOK

If your entire experience in French class was limited to fantasizing over Mireille (you know, the hot chick from those old *French in Action* instruction videos), you'll have a hard time doing much with this book. *Dirty French* was written with the assumption that you already know enough French to get by. After all, this is a slang book, and slang tends to be the last thing you learn after getting down all the basic (and relatively useless) sayings, such as "I live in the red house" and "Yes, I like the library very much, thank you." So, this isn't a beginner's grammar book. This is a book designed to take your French to the next level.

The chapters and explanations are set up, however, so that even with just a little French in your murky past, you should be able to call out any Jean-Pierre who starts killing your buzz with some Merlot-induced rant about how the CIA really blew up the Twin Towers. You'll find all your ammunition here, arranged by subject, chapter after chapter.

The slang included here is totally up to date, the kind of stuff you'd hear on the streets of Paris today. Except in special cases, the English is given first, followed by the French. Sometimes the French is given with alternatives—*laid(e)*, *mon/ma*—to

PRONOUNCING FRENCH)))

Here's a brief refresher on pronunciation. This is not how to name the letters of the alphabet but how to pronounce them when they appear in words.

A, à = *ah*

B = *bay*

C = *kah* (before "a, o, u"), *say* (before "e, i")

Ç = *say*

D = *day*

E, è = *euh* (like the second "e" in "telephone")

É = *ay*

F = *eff*

G = *gg* (before "a, o, u"), *zhee* (before "e, i")

H = [silent]

I = *ee*

J = *zhay*

K = *kah*

L = *elle*

M = *emm*

N = *enn*

O, ô = *oh*

P = *pay*

Q = *keww*

R = *airr*

S = *esse*

T = *tay*

U = *eww* (shape your mouth like a chicken's asshole— *un cul de poule*— and you'll say it right)

V = *vay*

X = *eeks*

Y = *ee*

Z = *z*

Je = *zheuh* (like the "ge" in "garage")

Tu = *tew*

Il, ils = *eel* (they're pronounced exactly the same; context is what let's people know when it's plural)

Elle, elles = *elle* (you might want to check the explanation right above)

On = *ohhhn*

Nous = *nou*

Vous = *voo* (like "voodoo")

The hardest thing for Americans to pronounce is the vowels. That's because we Americans flatline our sentences in monotones, and aren't used to pronouncing words with different emphasis. To get the hang of a good French pronunciation, you'll have to start by getting in touch with your inner Inspecteur Clouseau and speaking with a dramatic French accent: "Hey dude, ya wanna go get high?" would become "hAAY dewwwd, yoooo waaahn toooo gooo geeet hIII?" Don't worry, you'll get the hang of it.

account for gender differences. As we said before, this isn't a grammar book and you're not an idiot, so we expect that you'll be able to figure it out without any more explanation than that.

One important reminder: Slang is situational, and the slang in this book can get pretty hard-core. Use it at the wrong time or place and you'll find yourself in a bad situation (think Eddie Murphy walking into the biker bar in *48 Hours* and yelling out, "Whey' all da white wimmin at?"). So only use these expressions with people your own age, in situations where you know what's going on.

Now take your *Dirty French* and get dirty with it!

CHAPTER 1

HOWDY FRENCH
SALUTATIONS FRANÇAISES

•••••Hello
Bonjour

You probably shouldn't use French slang with strangers, especially if they're over 30, unless you want to get on their nerves right away. So when in doubt stick with the classic "Bonjour." After you get to know someone a little better, feel free to use some of these slangier expressions. (As for women, you'll get all kinds of attention if you try these with people you don't know.)

Hi
Salut

Hey!/Yo!
Ho!

Hey, you/Hey, baby
Coucou

Yo, dudes/guys!
Oh, les gars!

Yo, girls!
Oh, les filles!

On the telephone:

Hello?
Âllo?

Hey!
Salut!

·····Good morning/Good evening
Bonjour/Bonsoir

In French there are a bunch of informal variations on "good morning" and "good evening" for you to choose from.

Mornin', honey!
Bonjour, mon chéri (to a man)/*Bonjour, ma chérie* (to a woman)

Hey, babe—good morning!
Bonjour, toi!

Mornin'!
'Jour!

Evenin'!
'Soir!

Night!
Bonne nuit!

·····The hello kiss
La bise

You probably know that the French greet each other with little pecks on the cheek, like pigeons doing a mating dance. This is the local equivalent of the American "college hug" (which the French think is weird—they'll feel like you're coming on to them if you even try it).

TEXT MESSAGING—TEXTER)))

Text messaging has led to whole new ways of writing things by abbreviation:

Later	A+	(à plus)
Catch you later	A12C4	(à un de ces quatre)
LOL	MDR	(Mort de rire; "dying laughing")
Screw you	TG	(Ta gueule)
My ass	(.)	(Mon cul)
Kiss my ass	JTMD	(Je t'emmerde)
Go fuck yourself	VTFF	(Va te faire foutre)

Women exchange these kisses with all friends, male and female, when seeing them for the first time each day. If you kiss one person in a group, you should kiss them all (as long as they're roughly your age). And just go cheek to cheek and smooch the air; don't actually touch your lips to them.

Things are a bit different for men, who only use this kiss to greet female friends and their family. Among male friends, they simply shake hands.

Let's shake.
On se serre la main.

Should we hug?
On s'embrasse?

I'll kiss "hello."
Je te fais la bise.

"Kisses" (like on the phone or a postcard)
Bisous; bises

Kiss me on the mouth.
Embrasse-moi sur la bouche.

Do you wanna French kiss?
On se roule une pelle?
Literally, "to roll in a shovel." The word *baiser* is a real problem
in French. Traditional dictionaries will tell you that it's a kiss—but
that's only in older French. Today, *baiser* means to fuck or to
screw, both in the sexual sense ("I fucked your mom") or in the
mess-someone-up sense ("I fucked up your face").

·····What's up?
Quoi de neuf?

In English, when asked "what's up?" we usually give a one-
word answer because, let's face it, over here nobody really
cares. But in France they'll assume you actually want to
know how they're doing, and they'll expect you to give a real
answer, too. But stop short of mentioning how much it burns
when you pee.

How's it goin'?
Ça va?

How you doin'?
Tu vas bien?

You doin' good today?
T'es en forme?

Long time, no see!
Ça fait longtemps, dis donc!

Watcha up to?
Qu'est-ce que tu me racontes?

> **Nothing much.**
> *Pas grand chose.*
>
> **Same shit, different day.**
> *Comme d'hab'.*
>
> **How you been?**
> *Alors, qu'est-ce que tu deviens?*
>
> **So-so.**
> *Comme ci, comme ça.*

Same as always, man.
Ben, toujours pareil.

Good!
Ça roule!

Great!
Ça gaze!

Just peachy.
J'ai la pêche!

Awesome!
Ça baigne!

Unstoppable!
Je pète le feu
Literally, "I'm fartin' fire"

How's it hanging?
Qu'est-ce que tu fabriques?

It's hanging.
On se débrouille.

What's the word?
Quelles sont les nouvelles?

Same old bullshit.
Toujours le même bordel.

What the hell are you up to?
Qu'est-ce que tu fous?

What the hell are you doing here?
Qu'est-ce que tu fous là?

·····Bye!
Au revoir!

There are a bunch of slangy ways to tell someone that you're taking off.

Bye.
Bye; Salut.

See ya.
Ciao.
Young people often use the
Italian phrase.

Later.
À plus.

Catch you later.
À un de ces quatre.

See ya on the flip side.
À demain.

Call me.
On s'appelle.

Let's roll.
On bouge; On y va.

I'm out of here.
Je me casse.

Send me an e-mail/an IM.
Balance-moi un mél/un SMS; un texto.

·····Yo!
Oh!

The following expressions work really well to get people's
attention.

Look!
Regarde!

Check that out!
Regarde-moi ça!

Hey, kid!
Oh, jeune!
In the South around Marseille people say, "*Oh, minot!*"

Hey, babe!
Salut, ma beauté!

C'mere for a sec.
Viens voir une minute.
In this case, the French generally use "minute" instead of "second."

I gotta tell you something.
J'ai un truc à te dire.

If you are sitting outside (on "*la terrasse*") at a nice café and want to get the waiter's attention, we strongly recommend:

Please, Sir/Madam
Monsieur/Madame, s'il vous plaît!

If you want them to know that you're an American traveling in France for the first time and you'd like crappy, endlessly slow service, we strongly recommend:

Boy!/Dude!
Garçon!

Hey, get your fat ass over here!
Ho, tu te ramènes avec ton gros cul?

·····Sorry
Désolé(e)

French people aren't as quick to apologize as Americans, because the French **would rather die** ("*plutôt crever!*") than admit any wrongdoing. But if they do apologize, they will say the following (though deep inside they probably won't mean a word of it).

I'm sorry.
Je suis désolé(e).

I'm truly sorry.
Je suis vraiment désolé(e).; Je suis navré(e).

Sorry I'm late.
Je suis désolé(e) d'être en retard.

Sorry for crapping in your bidet.
Désolé d'avoir chié dans le bidet.

Pardon me.
Pardon.

My bad.
Désolé.; Autant pour moi.

Apologies.
Toutes mes excuses.

I fucked up!
J'ai merdé!

In the true French way, if you want to commiserate with someone without admitting any wrongdoing, try out one of these phrases:

That's the way it goes.
Ben, c'est comme ça.

That sucks!
Ça craint!

That's fucked up!
C'est dégueulasse!

ÏNTRODUCÏNG YOURSELF)))

SE PRÉSENTER

What's your name?
C'est quoi, ton nom?; Comment tu t'appelles?

My name's Jen.	*Je m'appelle Jen.*
I'm from the U.S.	*Je suis américaine.*
Yes, these are real breasts,	*Oui, ce sont de vrais seins,*
and stop staring at them	*et arrête de les mater*
before I slam your face.	*avant que je t'en mette une.*

*****

I'm Brad.	*Je suis Brad.*
I'm from Colorado, and I'm	*Je viens du Colorado, et je suis*
hung like a horse.	*pendu comme un âne.*

The French believe that donkeys *(ânes)* have bigger dicks than horses *(chevaux)*. Why they've spent time thinking about this, we don't know.

But I only slept with her once!
Mais je ne l'ai baisée qu'une fois!

Whoops! You're not my boyfriend.
Zut! T'es pas mon mec.

You poor thing.
Pauvre petit(e).

Shitty luck!
Pas de bol!; Manque de bol!

Ouch!
Aie!

Oh, shit!
Merde!

·····Excuse me
Excusez-moi

Politeness in France is mostly for work situations, between strangers, or when there's an age difference. With friends you can usually assume everything's fine. But between foreign languages and new cultures, misunderstandings happen pretty easily. So, without being a total dweeb about it, you might want to keep some of these tension-defusing phrases handy.

'Scuse me.
Excusez-moi. (formal or plural)/*Excuse-moi.* (casual)

Don't worry 'bout it.
T'inquiète.

Don't worry 'bout him/her.
Ignore-le/la.

Drop it, let's drop it.
Laisse béton.

'Scuse my shitty French.
Excuse mon français merdique.

Pardon my French!
Pardon, ça m'a échappé.

Can I get by here?
Ça te dérange pas si je passe?

Ever notice how nothing gets somebody angrier than asking them why they're so upset? So if you want to get somebody all worked up, just point out how unreasonable they're being.

Chill out!
Du calme!; Calmos!

Chill! I didn't do it on purpose!
Putain, ça va, j'ai pas fait exprès.

Don't get all worked up.
Te monte pas le mou!

Get over it.
C'est bon, y'a pas mort d'homme.

Don't get your panties in a wad!
On va pas en faire tout un fromage.

Don't shit your pants!
Te chie pas!

Can I at least get a word in?
Je peux en placer une?

•••••Please
S'il te plaît/S'il vous plaît

If you need something, there are many ways of asking—some more polite than others.

Yo! Over here!
S'iouplaît!

Can I get a little help?
Y a quelqu'un?

Why don't you call me sometime?
Appelle-moi. ; Téléphone-moi.

I'm on my knees.
Je suis à tes pieds.

I won't forget.
Je m'en rappellerai.

I owe you one.
Je te revaudrai ça.

I'm begging you.
Je t'en supplie.

I'm begging you to get your knee off my balls.
Je te supplie d'enlever ton genou de mes couilles.

Could you do me a favor?
J'ai un service à te demander.

Could you do me a favor and tell your friend I think she's hot?
Tu pourrais pas me rendre service et dire à ta copine que je la trouve hyper bonne?

Later, you can drop the niceties and tell them what you really want:

Do the dishes.
Fais la vaisselle.

Fix me something to eat.
Fais-moi à bouffer.

Clean up this mess.
Nettoie-moi ce bordel.

You should…
Tu devrais…

> **buy another round**
> *payer une autre tournée*
>
> **try a cocktail**
> *essayer un cocktail*
>
> **go topless**
> *enlever le haut*
>
> **not wear those shorts in public**
> *pas porter ce short en public*

·····Making friends
Soyons amis

Unlike in America, where it's common to talk to strangers in a bar or at school, in France people aren't used to this and will probably get a bit creeped out if you try it. Of course, this only applies to men—women are always welcome to walk up and introduce themselves. It just makes things so much easier. But generally in France, the best way to meet people is through groups rather than trying to go solo.

Nice to meet you.
Enchanté(e).

This is my first time in France.
C'est la première fois que je viens en France.

I'd like to meet some French people.
Je veux rencontrer des Français.

I don't understand French.
Je capte rien en français.

I don't understand a word you're saying.
Je pige que dalle.

This is my buddy.
C'est mon pote.

Can you please tell your buddy that I think he's cute.
Tu peux dire à ton pote que je le trouve mignon.

Your girlfriend's hot.
Ta copine est vraiment bonne.

I love your boyfriend's hairy chest.
J'adore la poitrine poilue de ton mec.

Are you by yourself?
T'es toute seule?

What do you do in your free time?
Qu'est-ce que t'aimes faire?

Teach me some cuss words.
Apprends-moi des gros mots.

I like hanging with you.
J'aime passer du temps avec toi.

Can I bum a smoke?
Tu peux me filer une clope?

Is that your dad?
C'est ton père, ce mec?

How old are you?
T'as quel âge?

Me, 30!? No way, it's just that we slept in the train station last night.
Moi, trente ans?! Mais non, c'est qu'on a créché à la gare hier soir!

Do you come here often?
Tu viens souvent ici?

·····Tourist gadgets
Matos du touriste

The French aren't all that camera crazy, and have some negative stereotypes about people who take tons of pictures in public places. But this attitude is starting to change, especially among the younger, tech-savvy crowd. Here are some useful terms and phrases.

A camera
Un appareil-photo

A digital camera
Un appareil-photo numérique; un numérique

A photo album
Un album photo

A camcorder
Un camescope

A DVD player
Un lecteur DVD

A cell phone
Un portable

Let's take a picture.
On prend une photo?

Can you take a picture of me?
Tu peux me prendre en photo?

I'm a photographer for a top model agency and would like to photograph you.
Je suis photographe de mode et je travaille pour de grandes agences. Je peux te prendre en photo?

Nudity is really trendy right now!
La nudité c'est vraiment tendance!

No thanks, porn doesn't do it for me.
Non merci, les photos de cul, c'est pas mon truc.

Don't ask your models in France to say "cheese!" Instead, tell them that a little bird is about to come out of the camera—this goes back to the early days when cameras looked like magician's boxes. But beware of French guys who randomly tell you that the big bird *(le gros oiseau)* is about to come out. They're not talking about photography.

Get ready! **The little bird** is about to come out!
*Attention! **Le petit oiseau** va sortir!*
You can say the same thing to tell someone that their fly is down.

CHAPTER 2

FRIENDLY FRENCH
LE FRANÇAIS AMICAL

·····Friends
Les amis

Unlike in America, where the best way to make "friends" is by telling someone that their MySpace pic is TOTALLY HOT!!!, in France the people are old-fashioned or antisocial or something, and they want to, like, actually know you first. Whatever. But if you do break through and make a French friend, they'll stick with you.

A buddy, a pal
un/une copain(e); un/une pote
Copain and *copine* can be confusing. *"Mon copain"* means "boyfriend," while *"un copain"* just means "a buddy."

My buddy lives around here.
Mon pote habite près d'ici.

A friend
Un/une ami(e)

Good friends are hard to find.
De bons amis sont difficiles à trouver.

Best friend
Meilleur ami/meilleure amie

> **Who's your best friend?**
> *C'est qui, ton meilleur ami?*

A school friend
Un/une camarade de classe

> **Do you keep in touch with your old school friends?**
> *Tu gardes le contact avec tes anciens camarades de classe?*

An acquaintance
Un/une connaissance

> **There's this acquaintance I want you to meet.**
> *J'ai une connaissance à te présenter.*

My boyfriend
Mon mec; mon copain

> **My boyfriend has huge feet.**
> *Mon mec a d'énormes pattes.*

My man
Mon homme

> **My man can't clean the dishes to save his life.**
> *Mon homme pourrait pas faire la vaisselle si sa vie en dépendait.*

My girlfriend
Mon amie; ma poule; ma nana; ma copine

> **My girlfriend is the sweetest thing.**
> *Ma copine, elle est la plus adorable de toutes.*

My dear
Mon chéri/ma chérie

> **Cup o' tea, my dear?**
> *Une tasse de thé, mon chéri?*

Roommate
Camarade de chambre

> **My roommate is a smelly asshole.**
> *Mon camarade de chambre est un connard infect.*

Dorms in France are mostly for foreign students. In big cities, though, high rents mean that more and more young people are sharing apartments. It's just like *Friends*—only poor, French, and not funny.

Housemate
Un/une colocataire; un/une coloc'

> **Your housemate is cute.**
> *Ton/Ta coloc' est mignon(ne).*

Coworker
Un/une collègue de travail

> **Do you have any French coworkers?**
> *Avez-vous des collègues français?*

·····Cool, funny shit
Des trucs fendards et cools

These expressions may be used in various contexts for things you like or think are funny, though the French don't laugh in public as much (or as loudly) as most Americans.

I know a **nice** little restaurant.
*Je connais un petit restau **sympa**.*

That bar has a **cool** dub band.
*Ce bar a un groupe de dub **cool**.*

Your little brother can **hold his own**.
*Ton frangin **assure comme mec**.*

Your kid sister can **hold her own**.
*Ta frangine **assure comme nana**.*

Daft Punk's last album is **great**.
*Le dernier disque de Daft Punk est **géant**.*

The production is **perfect**.
*La prod' est **impec'**.*

Your roommate is **a crack-up**.
*Ton/Ta camarade de chambre est **rigolo(te)**.*

Your stupid jokes are **hysterical**.
*Tes blagues à la con sont **hilarantes**.*

That commercial makes me **lose my shit**!
*Cette pub me fait **délirer grave**!*

You crazy asshole! Stop with the **jokes**! I'm gonna **piss my pants**.
*Enfoiré! Arrête tes **conneries**! Je vais **pisser dans mon froc**.*

·····Conversation starters
Briser la glace

While the French may have a centuries-old elite culture, highbrow references to Voltaire and Rimbaud won't get you very far if you're trying to make friends or get laid. Much better to settle for good ol' flattery and inane conversation.

I love your accent.
J'adore ton accent.

What's that perfume you're wearing?
C'est quoi, ton parfum?

FRENCH GOSSIP)))

The French love to chill out at cafés and gossip about people. It's sort of a national sport, and slang plays a big part in it.

He/She is...	Il/Elle est...
a stand-up guy	*un mec droit; un type correct*
a sweet girl	*une nana gentille*
a skank	*une pouffiasse; une salope*
a moron	*un abruti*
an airhead	*une conne*
a kiss-ass	*un/une fayot(te)*
a brown-noser	*un lèche-cul* [literally, "a butt-licker"]
a show-off	*un frimeur/une frimeuse; un m'as-tu vu*
a whiner	*un/une geignarde(e)*
a manic-depressive	*un/une cyclothymique*
a good-for-nothing	*un/une vaurien (ne); un/une fainéant(e)*
filthy rich	*plein(e) aux as; bourré(e) de fric*
dirt poor	*crève-la-dèche*

You look great in those jeans.
Comme tu assures dans ces jeans.

Do you prefer steak or seafood?
Tu préfères un steak ou des fruits de mer?

Can I buy you a drink?
Je peux t'offrir un verre?

Have we met before?
On s'est déjà rencontré?

You have the most beautiful eyes.
T'as les plus beaux yeux que j'ai jamais vus.

Want to see my tattoo?
Tu veux voir mon tatouage?

Would you like to come back to my place?
Tu veux rentrer avec moi?

Our babies would be gorgeous.
On ferait vraiment de très beaux bébés.

Are you sure you're 18?
T'es sûr/sure que tu as dix-huit ans?

·····Formalities
Les formalités

Watch out for a few cultural differences here. First, only medical doctors use "Dr." with their names; a Ph.D. in ceramics won't get you any special title. Second, there is no French equivalent to "Ms."; there are only "Mademoiselle" and "Madame." So the rule of thumb is to use "Mademoiselle" for every woman who looks under thirty; that won't get you into trouble.

Sir
Monsieur

Ma'am
Madame

Miss, Ms.
Mademoiselle

Dr.
Docteur

Mr. President
Monsieur le président

Judge
Monsieur/Madame le juge

When you get on better terms, you have some more informal options, too.

The doc
Le toubib

A cop
Un flic; un keuf

Ol' man Dumas
Le père Dumas

The boss
Le patron; le chef

Captain (sarcastic)
Le commandant
As in *Oui, mon commandant,* when your boyfriend orders you
around as if you were actually gonna listen.

·····Family
La famille

The concept of family remains pretty strong in France,
especially in the South. People tend to be close to their
entire family, including all the extended relatives, and kids
often live with their parents well into adulthood until they get
married or finally move in with their partners. But the French
are slowly Americanizing: More and more they come home
after a few years, divorced and with a couple of kids in tow,
to move back with their folks. Isn't it nice to see how much
we have in common?

Daddy
Papa

> **My daddy's a fireman.**
> *Mon papa est pompier.*

Mommy
Maman

> **My mommy likes to tickle me.**
> *Ma maman aime me faire des chatouilles.*

My old man
Mon vieux; mon vioque

> **My old man farts like a bastard.**
> *Mon vieux pète comme un salaud.*

My old lady
Ma vieille; ma vioque

> **My old lady's got a tough life.**
> *Ma vioque a la vie dure.*
> In the U.S., "my old lady" refers to your wife; in France, it's
> your mom. In both countries, it's best when they're not the
> same person.

Stepdad/Stepmom
Beau-père/Belle-mère
These are the same words for "father-in-law" and "mother-in-law."

> **My stepdad really cramps my style.**
> *Mon beau-père me pourrit vraiment la vie.*

My bro'
Mon frangin

> **My brother doesn't do shit.**
> *Mon frangin est un glandeur.*

My sis'
Ma frangine

> **Call my sis' a whore again and I'll kill you.**
> *Si tu traites encore ma frangine de pute, je te tue.*

·····Characters
Figures

Kids
Les enfants

> **Kids are so cute.**
> *Les enfants sont tellement mignons.*

Teens
Les ados

> **Teens smell bad.**
> *Les ados puent grave.*

Wino
Le pochetron; le poivrot

> **Don't let the wino puke on you.**
> *Fais gaffe que le pochetron te vomisse pas dessus.*

Bum
Le/la clochard(e); le/la clodo; le/la SDF

> **It's good karma to give money to bums.**
> *Ça porte bonheur de donner des sous aux clodos.*

Dirty old man
Le vieux dégueulasse

That dirty old man honked my boob on the subway.
Ce vieux dégueulasse m'a empoigné le nibard dans le métro.

A badass
Le loubard

He's a real badass.
Ça c'est un vrai loubard.

A thug
Un voyou

Your brother's a thug.
Ton frère est un voyou.

Spoiled rich kid
Un fils/une fille à papa

I hate spoiled rich kids.
Je déteste les fils à papa.

Ladies' man
Un tombeur; un homme à femmes

That idiot thinks he's a ladies' man.
Cet idiot se prend pour un tombeur.

Good ol' boy (in a positive sense)
Un bon bougre

He's a regular good ol' boy.
C'est un vrai bon bougre.

Redneck
Un pequenot; un blaireau
From the animal "badger"

Goddamn racist redneck!
Putain de pequenot raciste!

Country hick
Un plouc

That country hick knows culture about as well as my dog.
Ce plouc est aussi cultivé que mon chien.

Jock
Le sportif/la sportive

> **That jock has a soccer ball for a brain.**
> *Ce sportif a un ballon de foot à la place du cerveau.*

Horndog
Le queutard

> **That horndog has a dick where his brain should be.**
> *Ce queutard a une bite à la place du cerveau.*

Horny slut
La traînée

> **That horny slut is always ready to go.**
> *Cette traînée a toujours le feu au cul.*

•••••Everyday folks
Le commun des mortels

Each country has its own stereotypes that the media and public use all the time. Here are a few clues about French stereotypes, so that you'll recognize whom you're dealing with.

White trash
Les beaufs
Being white trash isn't so much a question of money as it is of style—though usually they don't have much of either. For the guys, they have only one obsession that doesn't involve alcohol or ass: their car. The "*beauf*" has a strong preference for French automakers and cars (especially the old, boxy Renault 12 of the '70s, or a used Peugeot 405 from the '90s). He spends most of his salary (if he works at all) on accessories to make his car "unique," many of which are borrowed from the U.S.: hanging dice, fake fur covering the steering wheel, top-of-the-line car stereo with speakers taking up the entire trunk. When he hits his midlife crisis, he'll prefer a ponytail to the American

mullet, but he'll unbutton his shirt to show tufts of hair and fake gold chains, and will sport some bun-hugger pants. He's convinced he's a player, so he goes heavy on the French version of Old Spice (Drakkar Noir). He usually can't be bothered to talk to his girlfriend, but he'll start a fight if anybody else tries to. He has a favorite bar, and is incredibly loyal in friendship…when he's not drunk and trying to bust a bottle over your head.

The Bible-thumpers
Les culs bénis
Literally, these are the "holy asses," also known as "*les bigots*" (fire and brimstone dads) and "*les bigotes*" (church ladies). These French believers, usually Catholic, are fanatical in their faith. They're starting to make a comeback, though percentage-wise there are more atheists in France than in the U.S., and the fastest-growing religion is Islam. The *culs bénis* go to mass every week, prepare for Communion, volunteer at their parish, attend private Catholic schools, and join the Boy Scouts or Girl Scouts.

The commuters
Les métro-boulot-dodo
Making fun of these people is kind of harsh, because it's a hard life. You wake up at 5 a.m. in your small, suburban apartment while it's still dark outside. You get dressed, grab a coffee, walk 15 minutes to the regional train, stand in the onboard crowd for 30 minutes, transfer to the subway (*métro*), take it for another 45, and soon you're at your desk for another day at the job (*boulot*). Nine hours later, reverse paths, microwave a frozen dinner, watch the news, and hit the sack to snooze (*dodo*, from "*dormir*," to sleep). At the same time, though, when you see them asleep on the train with their heads all the way back and their mouths wide open, it's tempting to imagine what would happen if you dropped a goldfish down the hatch.

Hippies
Les baba cools
The '60s were a big deal in France, probably even more so than in the U.S. The student movement of May 1968 almost brought down the government. Many of the kids who participated in and drove the movement are still around today, easily recognizable by their hippy

accessories (incense, beads, tie-dye dresses, long hair). But you probably won't see too many because they avoid the cities.

The cow pies
Les bouseux
These are the farmers who come into town and stand next to you in line at the bank. Even if you don't see them coming, you can smell them: "*Une bouse*" is a cow pie, so they're called "*bouseux*" because of the cow shit splashed all the way up their rubber boots. They're the last symbols of old France, with accents that make a barefoot Kentucky minister sound like an Oxford grad, and driving habits that make a tractor on the highway seem fast.

The bo-hos
Les bobos
Most of these bohemian "68ers" ("*soixante-huitards*") did eventually get tired of eating grain cereals, grooving on sitar music, and living out of a VW bus. And, surprisingly, many of them ended up getting quite wealthy. They've been divorced several times, and the moms want to be best friends with their daughters, and the dads want to sleep with girls their daughters' age. At the same time, though, they see themselves as enlightened and cultured, with esoteric spiritual beliefs and an absolute devotion to recycling. The politically conscious *bobos* usually have an eccentric signature, like Rollerblading to work, and they belong to what's known as the "Gauche caviar"—left-wingers who speak with great passion about the suffering of the poor…while eating caviar in their spectacular Parisian duplex apartments.

The rich folk
Les costume-cravate
Literally the "suit and ties," who often are graduates of French or American business schools, they are executives ("*les cadres*") employed by corporations. It's never been terribly cool to talk about how much money you make or to splash it around in people's faces, but *les costume-cravate* are trying to change that. Often pretentious, individualist, and driven by money only, they are so wrapped up in their success that they won't notice (or won't care) if you bang their wife or husband.

The upper crust

Les bourges

Some of the *costume-cravate* join the ranks of the *bobos* when they turn fifty; terrified of getting old, they suddenly discover a passion for windsurfing, travel to Third World countries, and switch to solar power. The others consolidate their money into social prestige by veering conservative: They become "*bourges*" (short for "*bourgeois*"). They'll do everything possible to smell like old money, and will disdain anyone who got rich the way they did. The fathers will be disciplinarians, the mothers uptight and formal. It's not easy to grow old gracefully when you're rich—but it probably still beats being poor.

CHAPTER 3

PARTY FRENCH
LE FRANÇAIS FESTIF

Frankly, if you don't see any use for this chapter you're probably too busy playing *World of Warcraft*. Hopefully your avatar has better social skills than you do.

·····What's the plan?
C'est quoi, le plan?

Do you have **plans** tonight?
*T'as des **projets** ce soir?*

You goin' out?
Tu sors?

What're you doin'?
Tu fais quoi?

Are you busy tonight?
Tu fais quelque chose ce soir?

I'm bored shitless.
***Je me fais chier** comme c'est pas possible.*

Let's **have a drink** somewhere.
*Allons **boire un coup** quelque part.*

This place **sucks**.
*C'est **nul** ici.*

This place looks dangerous.
Ça craint ici.

Should we go?
On bouge?

Should we get out of here?
On se tire?

Should we blow this joint?
On se casse?

Don't be such a buzz kill.
Ne nous casse pas les couilles!
Literally, "don't bust our balls"

Why do French guys always **check themselves out** in the mirror when they dance?
*Pourquoi les mecs français **se regardent** tous danser dans les miroirs?*

·····Party!
C'est la fête!

The French have more ways to say "party" than the ancient Greeks had gods. For starters, there's *la fête, la bringue, la java, la noce, la bomba, la nouba, la bamboche, la bamboula, la fiesta, la teuf, la ribote, la goguette, la ribouldingue*…. Some French parties get so debauched that they make those MTV Spring Breaks look like your stepmom's Easter potluck. So arm yourself by mastering the following party words.

Party animal
Un fêtard; un bringueur; un noceur

I feel like **partying**!
*Je suis d'humeur à **faire la fête**!*

I'm up for anything.
***Je suis prêt(e)** à tout.*

I wanna **have a great time** tonight.
*Je veux **m'éclater** ce soir.*

I'm gonna **let loose!**
*Je vais **me déchaîner!***
Literally, "get unchained"

I'm fed up with beer. Let's go dancing for once.
***J'en ai marre** de la bière.*
Allons danser pour une fois.

Let's go to a **club**.
*Allons en **boîte**.*

This place is happenin'.
Ça chauffe ici.

That's a **badass groove!**
*C'est un **putain de groove**, ça!*

Damn, girl, your body is bangin'!
Oh cousine, chaud devant!

Let's get it on!
On attaque!

·····Getting down
Mettre le feu

The minimum drinking age in France is 18, but no one actually pays attention to it. As long as you can see over the counter, you can buy booze. Same thing with clubs. As long as you're dressed right and looking good, the bouncer will let you in, regardless of age. And most places stay open all night, so there's no need to pound your weight in Goldschläger the second you make it to the bar.

Let's get down!
Mettons le feu!
Literally, "let's get it lit"

Let's do an **all-nighter**.
*Faisons **nuit blanche***
Literally, a "white night," or they stayed out until it was light again

Want **another drink**?
*Tu veux **un autre verre**?*

Wanna go home with me?
Tu veux rentrer avec moi?

Let's…

    hit on some guys
    branchons des mecs

    hit on some girls
    branchons des gonzesses/des filles/des nanas

    get some play
    allons tâter de ça

    get laid (with a guy)
    allons nous taper des mecs

    get laid (with a girl)
    allons nous taper des gonzesses/des filles/des nanas

If you're at a French club and some fugly schmo starts hitting on you, don't make eye contact and *definitely* don't flash a smile. What is only a polite hello in the U.S. translates to "come and get it" in Paris or Bordeaux.

·····Where French people get down
Où les Français sortent

Bars and pharmacies are the most common businesses found in a typical French city. Seriously, it's bizarre how many pharmacies there are in France. It's like everyone has cheap health care that pays for their drugs or something. Oh wait, they do.

    Let's go to…
    Allons à/au/dans…

        a bar
        un bar

a bar-tobacco shop
un bar-tabac
A great place where you can get your drink on while smoking all manner of fine tobacco products. Somewhere in Virginia, Philip Morris is smiling in his grave.

a pub or tavern
un pub; un pub irlandais

a wine bar
un bar à vins

a café
un café
Café refers to either the drink (coffee) or the place, or both.
A cool thing about cafés in France is that they always have beer on tap, as well as a small bar, and it's usually cheaper to drink there.

a café-theater
un café-théâtre
You can eat and drink there, but you can also buy a ticket for a comedy play or standup act.

a music bar
un café-concert
Usually jazz, traditional French music, or World Music, with high cover or drink prices.

a cabaret
un cabaret
Your ticket includes a Vegas-style show and, depending on the place, a meal and/or Champagne.

a nightclub
une boîte de nuit; un night-club
More discreet and quiet than a disco, often private

a whore bar
an bar à putes

a rave
une rave

the "afters"
l'after

a sandwich hut/trailer/kiosk
une baraque; un kiosque à sandwichs
Usually where you will find yourself at 3 a.m. waiting for some *merguez*, a spicy lamb sandwich

an "American-style" bar
un bar américain
This is a special kind of bar with hostesses (*hôtesses*), who are basically in-house escort girls. Their job is to run up your tab as much as possible by ordering expensive bottles of Champagne. They love to rip off tourists and they have huge bouncers to make sure you forget about trying to get your money back. In other words, it's a really shitty place to hang out.

a swingers club
un club libertin; une boîte échangiste
These joints, with about fifty nekked people getting down in a series of rooms, are illegal in the U.S. and, well, kind of illegal in France. But they've become hangouts, especially in Paris, for jaded male celebrities looking for a thrill. So on any given night you might see a bunch of former child stars bumpin' uglies with a gaggle of Parisian "models" while some creepy guy in leather pants films it all from the corner.

> How about an **orgy** tonight in a swingers club?
> *Une **partouze** dans une boîte échangiste, ça vous dit pour ce soir?*

a disco
une boîte de nuit; la discothèque
French discos don't open until 11 p.m. at the earliest, but nobody really shows up until about 1. There's usually a pricey cover charge that includes a free drink, but women can negotiate to get in free. Getting in has nothing to do with age and everything to do with looks (and, unfortunately, sometimes race—some French discos have been closed for racial profiling). All French discos use bouncers to select the clientele and take care of security.

THE THREE "NEVERS" OF FRENCH DISCOS)))

1. **Never** show up at the door in a group of all guys.

2. **Never** show up wearing shorts or flip-flops (unless you're a woman).

3. **Never** assume you will be able to take a shit at a disco (it won't be possible, trust us).

Technically, a bouncer never actually rejects anyone. Instead, he asks if you've got the "club membership" or tells you that it's a private party. After that, though, if you bug him he'll probably make it easier for you to understand:

Look, you dress like an American. Now **get the fuck out of here** before I explode your face.
*Écoute, t'es sapé comme un gros ricain. Alors **casse-toi** avant que je t'explose la tête.*

You should **chill out**. When you get angry your face starts to look like my dick.
***Calme-toi**, vieux. Quand tu te fous en rogne, ça fait franchement tête de vier.*

Go fuck yourself. I'm about to kill you.
***Va te faire enculer**. Je vais te massacrer.*

Whatever. Shove **your membership card** up your ass, good and deep.
*Comme tu veux, mais **la carte de membre**, tu peux te la carrer dans le cul, bien profond.*

·····Boozing it up
Beuveries

France's love affair with wine means you can buy it pretty much anywhere, including great bottles at reasonable prices in supermarkets, which would be kinda like buying Dom Pérignon at your local 7-Eleven. Stay away, however, from those plastic bottles of wine. They're ridiculously cheap for a reason, and they make you regurgitate showers of pink chunder. Beer is more popular in the north and northeast of the country.

Cheers!
Santé! ; Tchin-tchin!

To good friends!
Aux amis!

To Napoleon, that midget asshole.
À Napoléon, ce con de nain!

You got beer on tap?
Vous avez des bières à la pression?

Gimme a...
Donne-moi...

> **beer**
> *de la bière*
>
> **cheap beer**
> *de la bibine*
>
> **glass of beer**
> *un demi, s'i' vous plaît*
>
> **pint**
> *un sérieux; une pinte*
>
> **liter of beer**
> *un litre*
> The French equivalent of the American 40
>
> **bottle opener**
> *un tire-bouchon*

Let's pound these shots.
On va se les faire cul sec.

Hey bartender, **a round** for my friends.
*M'sieu! **une tournée** pour mes amis.*

Chug! chug! chug!
Eh glou! eh glou! eh glou!

·····Wine
Vin

Who's buried in Grant's Tomb? Where does Champagne come from? French wines bear the name of the region where they're produced. Bordeaux in the southwest and Burgundy (Bourgogne) in the center are the most famous reds. But you can find some cheaper but still-solid reds from the Marseille region, Côtes du Rhône.

May I have a glass of...?
Puis-je avoir un verre de... ?

red wine
vin rouge

a small glass of red wine
un ballon de rouge

white wine
vin blanc

rosé wine
vin rosé

rotgut wine
pinard

Champagne, sparking wine
Champagne

Wine coolers don't exist in France but there is something called a "*kir*," which is wine mixed with other alcohol. The standard kir is 2/3 white wine (Bourgogne Aligoté) and 1/3 crème de cassis (black currant liqueur). There are a bunch of spin-offs and they're all delicious:

Kir normand
Cider with *crème de cassis*

Kir cardinal
Red Bordeaux with *crème de cassis*

Kir royal
Champagne with *crème de cassis*

Kir impérial
Champagne with *crème de framboise* (raspberry)

Le Double K
The Krushchev Kir (white wine, vodka, *crème de cassis*)

·····Booze
Bibine

Many French, especially in the countryside, still make their own brandy and cognac. If you're invited for dinner, your

DRiNKiNG SONGS)))

CHANSONS À BOIRE

One could write an entire book about French drinking songs. Here are a few of the classics that will certainly get you some attention with the natives:

C'est à boire qu'il nous faut!
C'est à boire, à boire, à boire,
C'est à boire qu'il nous faut,
Oh! Oh! Oh! Oh!

Something to drink is what we need!
Something to drink, to drink, to drink,
Something to drink is what we need!
Oh! Oh! Oh! Oh!

Boire un petit coup c'est agréable,
Boire un petit coup c'est agréable,
Boire un petit coup c'est doux,
Mais il ne faut pas rouler dessous la table.
Boire un petit coup c'est agréable,
Boire un petit coup c'est doux!

Having a little drink does us good,
Having a little drink does us good,
Having a little drink is nice,
But don't drink yourself under the table.
Having a little drink does us good,
Having a little drink is nice.

Chevaliers de la Table Ronde,
Chevaliers de la Table Ronde,
Goûtons voir si le vin est bon.
Chevaliers de la Table Ronde,
Goûtons voir si le vin est bon.
Goûtons voir, oui, oui, oui,
Goûtons voir, non, non, non,
Goûtons voir,
Si le vin est bon.
Goûtons voir, oui, oui, oui,
Goûtons voir, non, non, non,
Goûtons voir,
Si le vin est bon.

Knights of the Round Table,
Knights of the Round Table,
Let's see if the wine is any good.
Knights of the Round Table,
Let's see if the wine is any good.
Let's taste it, yes, yes, yes,
Let's taste it, no, no, no,
Let's see
If the wine is any good.
Let's taste it, yes, yes, yes,
Let's taste it, no, no, no,
Let's see
If the wine is any good.

host may bring some out at the end of the meal in a clear bottle with no label or just a taped-on piece of paper with a date scribbled on it. It'll have a pear or apricot floating at the bottom. Next to these concoctions, Mezcal tastes like candy. And it's *really* bad manners to wimp out, as it's the house tradition to enjoy with guests.

Pour me...
Versez-moi...

un pastis
You add a little water and an ice cube to an anis liqueur and the yellowish liqueur turns white. Drink a bunch of these and you'll have a blinding headache like you've never known.

un panaché
A lemonade beer tastes great, especially when it's hot or in the afternoon.

un despérado, un despy'
A beer with tequila in it

une eau-de-vie
Brandy

une Poire William
It takes 61 pounds of pears to make 2 liters of this pear brandy!

un Calvados
Apple brandy from Normandy

un Trou normand
This Calvados-type drink, which translates to "The Norman Hole," is a killer. After a really heavy meal, you're supposed to throw this burning mixture down the hatch in order to sear a hole through your just-digested food and make room for dessert. Try this once and you'll understand why so many people in the French countryside have cirrhosis.

If you're not man enough to shred your liver with a Norman Hole, you can always get mixed drinks and cocktails at nightclubs—though they're not as popular in France, and most bars don't serve them. Here are a few favorites:

une tequila frappée

For a tequila banger, mix tequila and tonic water, place a coaster over it, bang it on the table, and guzzle it down as it fizzes—chase with lime and salt.

un Kiss Cool

Curaçao and Sambuca in a shot glass. Swirl it around in your mouth as long as you can stand it (it'll burn), swallow it down, and then inhale the vapors.

le Vagin

"The Vagina" is a bit of lime juice in the bottom of a shot glass, a couple fingers of apricot brandy, and a maraschino cherry. Shoot it and bite into the cherry.

·····Totally wasted
Défoncé(e)

When you get to use the expressions in this section, it'll probably already be too late.

I'm starting to get…
Je commence à être…

> **a little tipsy**
> *un peu pompette*
> Mostly for girls

> **a bit drunk**
> *un peu saoul(e)*

> **buzzed**
> *bourré(e)*

> **sick**
> *malade*

That dumb tourist is…
Ce con de touriste est…

> **smashed**
> *fracassé(e)*

> **really trashed**
> *complètement défoncé(e)*

> **three sheets to the wind**
> *complètement dans les vapes; complètement à l'ouest*

about to puke
sur le point de gerber

I'm gonna get **ripped**!
*Je vais me **fracasser**!*

She's really **lit**!
*Elle est complètement **allumée**!*

We're so **fucked up**!
*On est complètement **défoncés**!*

Wow, did you see her **projectile-vomit**?!
*Waow, mais t'as vu ce **bouquet de gerbe**?!*

Last night I was so **wasted** I got up and peed on the sofa.
*Hier soir j'étais tellement **défoncée** que j'ai pissé debout sur le sofa.*

·····Taking it easy
Relaxation

After a few nights of nonstop partying in Nice or Lyon, you'll be glad to know the following phrases:

Tonight I...
Ce soir je...

> **am toast**
> *suis crevé(e)*
>
> am **going home** early
> *vais rentrer tôt*
>
> wanna **watch a DVD**
> *veux mater un DVD*
>
> wanna **catch a flick**
> *veux me faire un cinoche*
>
> am gonna **kick back**
> *vais me la filer tranquille*
>
> am gonna **chill out**
> *vais me la couler douce*
>
> am just **hangin' out** at home
> *traîne à la maison*

am not gonna do squat
vais rien foutre

am gonna just **jack around**
*vais **branler que dalle***

am gonna **dick off**
*vais **glander***

·····Weed
L'herbe

Paris is not Amsterdam when it comes to drugs. The French government cracks down pretty hard, and people are cautious about it on the streets. Nonetheless, a lot of French smoke weed and hash. A few grow it at home, but most comes from Morocco in North Africa. No guarantees on the quality. And, as everywhere else in the world, it pays to know your dealer. Bogus ones will try to screw you over and sell you mixtures of oregano and wax that will have you on the toilet all night.

A joint
Un joint; un oinj

A doobie
Un pétard; un beuze

A spliff
Un spliff

Hash
Le hasch; le haschisch; du shit

Weed
La fumette
Literally, "the small smoke," because French weed is weaker than hash

To grow marijuana
Faire pousser de la Marie-Jeanne

My aunt's **an old hippie**; she grows weed on her balcony.
*Ma tante est **une vieille baba cool**; elle fait pousser de la Marie-Jeanne sur son balcon.*

Do you know a **dealer**?
*Tu peux nous trouver **un dealer**?*

Are you holding?
T'as que'que chose pour nous?

Do you know where I can get some stuff?
Tu sais où je peux en avoir?

I'm getting a little **stoned**.
*Je commence à être un peu **défoncé(e)**.*

Shit, I'm really fucking **baked**. I'm gonna take a **nap**.
*Putain, je suis complètement **dans la ouate**. Je vais faire **un somme**.*

I've got the munchies something fierce.
Il faut absolument que je grignote quelque chose.

I was so high, I ate a pound of cookie dough.
***J'étais tellement à l'ouest**, j'ai bouffé 500 grammes de pâte à galettes.*

·····Hard stuff
La drogue dure

While smoking weed is somewhat tolerated in France, coke or Ecstasy will get you jail time. Definitely a case of "buyer beware." So if anybody asks, you didn't learn these words from us.

Coke
La coca

Crack
Le crack

White powder
La poudre blanche

A line
Une ligne

A rail
Un rail

To do a bump
Remettre ça

Heroin
L'héroïne

Horse
L'héro

To shoot up
Se shooter

> There's a bum outside **shooting up** some horse.
> *Dehors y a un clodo qui **se shoote** à l'héro.*

Pills
Des pilules

> We took some **pills** at the rave.
> *On a gobé des **pilules** à la rave.*

Man, you're an **addict**.
*Mon vieux, t'es **accro'**.*

Yeah, well, you're **a dope fiend**.
*Et toi, t'es un **accro' de la fumette**.*

Ecstasy, X
L'ecsta'

> She loves to screw on **ecstasy**.
> *Elle adore baiser à **l'ecsta**.*

CHAPTER 4

BODY FRENCH
LE FRANÇAIS DU CORPS

·····The French sexy
Le sexy français

The French ideal is not much different from other nationalities. But whereas the ideal American man is tall, dark, and handsome, the perfect Frenchman is blond and blue-eyed. French tastes in females are pretty standard: nice tits, small waist. Nothing unusual there.

He/She is...
Il/Elle est...

handsome (guys)
beau

beautiful (girls)
belle

cute
mignon(ne)

really cute (girls)
craquante

totally hot (girls)
bandante
Literally, "you'll get a hard-on just looking"; using the literal translation of "hot" (*chaude*) for a girl can also mean "horny")

totally hot (guys)
une gravure de mode

pretty (girls)
jolie

sexy
sexy

stylish
à la mode

really fashionable
glamour

hip
branché(e)
Literally, "plugged in," "connected"

BODY TYPES)))

TYPES DE CORPS

He is/She is...	Il est/Elle est...
tall	*grand(e)*
well-built (girls)	*bien foutue*
buff (guys)	*bien baraqué*
little/short	*petit(e)*
short	*court(e) sur pattes* ("short on their paws")
a midget	*un/une nain(e)*
frail (guys), delicate (girls)	*délicat(e)*
scrawny	*un sac d'os* ("bag of bones")
hunchback	*bossu(e)*
tanned	*bronzé(e)*
pale	*pale, palot*
long-haired	*chevelu(e)* (hippies, not cavemen)
hairy	*poilu(e)*
chunky, chubby	*grassouillet(te)*
fat	*gros/grosse*
skinny	*maigre; maigrichon(ne)*
anorexic	*squelettique*

trendy
tendance

He/She has...
Il/Elle a...

a lean **face**
*un **visage** fin*

a friendly or likeable **face**
*une bonne **piffe***

a good "**mug**"
*une bonne **gueule***

a square **jaw** (guys)
*un **visage** carré*

a hot **figure**
*une très belle **silhouette***

good **measurements**
*de bonnes **mensurations***

•••••The French nasty
La laideur française

If you're a sucker for those TV commercials that always show the French as ultrastylish and slim, you're in for a huge surprise. The ugly are a well-represented species in France.

He/She has...
Il/Elle a...

a round **face**
*la **tête** arrondie*

beady **eyes**
*de petits **yeux***

a fugly "**grill**"
*une **tronche** pas possible*

a stubby **body** and short **legs**
*un **corps** trapu et de petites **jambes***

a nasty **mop of hair**
*une sale **tignasse***

a bad **figure**
*un **physique** désagréable; mal **foutu(e)***

a tiny **head**
*une petite **tête***

a big **head**
*une grosse **tête***
To *have* a "big head" can mean that you're conceited, just as in English. But if you say that someone *is* a "big head," it means that they're either really smart or a total nerd.

a face made for smacking
*une **tête à** claques*
A great expression for people like Paris Hilton or Jim Carrey whose grins are so moronic that it spoils their looks.

Your girlfriend looks like a Perrier **bottle**.
*Ta copine ressemble à une **bouteille** de Perrier.*
The French way to say, "She has small tits and a big ass."

Your boyfriend has a **beer belly**.
*Ton mec a un **bébé Kro**.*
"Kro" is short for Kronenbourg, the most common brand of French beer. In English, this would be like saying, "He's expecting a baby Bud."

You gotta do something about those **love handles**.
*Il faut que tu perdes ces **poignets d'amour**.*
The French magazine *Paris-Match* once tried to curry favor with President Sarkozy by publishing a shirtless photo of him with his love handles Photoshopped out.

Her **head** is bigger than her **body**.
*Sa **tête** est plus grosse que son **corps**.*

Did you **comb your hair with a broom**?
*Tu t'es **coiffé avec un balai**?*

Look! It's the **bearded woman**.
*Regarde! C'est la **femme à barbe**.*

You could make a fur coat out of her **butt hair**.
*Tu pourrais te faire un manteau en fourrure avec ses **poils du cul**.*

He is/She is...
Il est/Elle est...

    ugly
    laid(e)

homely
un/une laideron(ne); un/une mocheté(e)

so ugly he/she **attracts animals**
*tellement laid(e) qu'il/elle **attire les bêtes***

slimy
un gros porc

dirty
sale

filthy
crade

a dog
un thon
Literally, "a tuna"

a fat sausage
un boudin

a nasty cow
une grognasse

repulsive (guys)
répugnant

beastly (guys)
ignoble

completely gross (guys)
immonde
Literally, "not of this world"

nasty (guys)
vilain

a fat mound (guys)
un gros tas

•••••The can
Les chiottes

There's nothing worse than being abroad and not knowing how to find a public toilet when you realize that the pâté was a day too old. In France, that may mean finding "Madame

Pipi" (literally, "the Pee Lady") and having to shell out a few coins, especially for a sit-down.

Where is/are...?
Où...?

the restrooms
sont les toilettes; les WC; les sanitaires

the john
est le petit coin

the toilet paper
est le papier cul
Literally, "butt paper"

the TP
est le PQ

the bathroom attendant
Madame Pipi
In tourist cities especially, it's common to have bathroom attendants charge at the entrance to restrooms in large public facilities (number two will cost you more). If you don't go to a place hosted by a Madame Pipi, the probability of finding any TP in a public restroom is equivalent to that of finding a diamond in your shit.

the "Turkish" toilets
les chiottes à la turque
Squat-and-shit toilets, common in older restaurants and bars, consist of a hole in the porcelain floor with two raised foot pads to stand on. Unless you're wearing rain gear, make sure you stand back up a bit when you pull the overhead chain to flush. And it gets worse: In many of these older toilets, the lights are on a timer. If you don't finish fast enough, you'll find yourself stranded, truly understanding the phrase *J'y vois comme dans **un trou du cul*** (It's as dark as **a butthole** in here).

the public toilet
les toilettes; le WC public
In main cities like Paris and Marseille, you'll find space-age bathrooms (tall, shiny cylinders) right in the middle of the sidewalk. You put your coins in the slot, the door

slides open, and you walk in. Do not—we repeat, do not—try to slide in after someone else to use it after them for free. After the door closes, it locks and there's an automatic cleaning process where you'll get doused and fumigated.

Don't go in there, some asshole **blew his ass out**.
Surtout n'entrez pas, y a un enculé qui s'est défoncé le trou du cul.

That's a shitty thing to say.
T'es chiant(e) de dire ça.

Betty thinks her shit doesn't stink.
Betty pète plus haut que son cul.
Literally, "Betty farts from higher than her asshole"

He thinks he's the shit.
Il se prend pas pour une merde.

You're a sack of shit.
Espèce de sac à merde.

I shit in your face. (i.e., Go fuck yourself)
Je te chie sur la gueule.

Eat shit.
Mange merde.

I don't have shit covering my eyes.
J'ai pas de la merde aux yeux.
As in, "I wasn't born yesterday."

STINKIN' IT UP)))

EMPESTER

When traveling in a foreign country, sometimes your friends forget to shower, and just about every part of their body can get pretty ripe. The expression "il pue de la..." allows you to add in whatever body part you need, to tell them just how stank they really are.

Bob pue des pieds.	Bob's **feet** stink.
Jean-Pierre pue du cul.	Jean-Pierre's **ass** smells nasty.
Pam pue de la chatte.	Pam's **pussy** is rank.
Gérard pue de la gueule.	Gérard's got **stink-breath**.

·····Shitting
Chier

When "nature calls" in France, it's just that: natural. Nobody is ashamed of pissing and shitting, the way they are in the U.S. When your French host starts to describe his or her digestion to you in great detail, you'll know you're part of the family.

You just stepped in **shit**!
*Tu viens de marcher dans la **merde**!*

I gotta...
Je dois...

> drop a **turd**
> *lâcher un **étron***

> make a **poo-poo**
> *faire **caca***

> **take a dump**
> *caguer; chier*

> **drop a bomb**
> *couler une bielle* (a rod); *couler un bronze*

> **wipe my ass**
> *me torcher le cul*

I've got a bitch of a need **to shit**.
*J'ai une putain d'envie de **chier**.*

I'm about to crap my pants.
Je vais me faire au froc.

I'm prairie-dogging it.
J'ai le cigare au bout des lèvres.
Literally, "the cigar is at the edge of my lips"

I just shit a **snake**. (a long, skinny turd)
*J'ai chié un **serpent**.*

That shit ripped my ass apart.
Je me suis défoncé le trou du cul.

That cassoulet gave me the runs/the shits.
Ce cassoulet m'a donné la chiasse.

You'll end up with **Montezuma's revenge** if you drink Paris **tap water**.
*Tu auras **la turista** si tu bois **l'eau du robinet** à Paris.*

Nothing better than a really good shit.
Rien de tel qu'une bonne grosse merde.

In fact, shitting is so great that at least one French proverb claims it's better than love:

Love may burn like fire, but the need to shit is the greatest desire.
L'amour est un feu qui dévore mais l'envie de chier est plus forte encore.

·····Burping and Farting
Roter et péter

English insults use a lot of sexual images ("Screw you," "I'll fuck you up"), while French insults tend toward the scatological. So all those ridiculous insults in *Monty Python and the Holy Grail*, like "I fart in your general direction," are actually barely tweaked but *real* French expressions.

SPECIALTY FARTS)))

PETS SPÉCIAUX

The SBD (silent but deadly)	*La louffe*
The skidmark fart	*Le pet foireux; le pet coulant*
The liquid fart	*Le pet liquoreux*
The mudslide fart	*Le pet merdeux*
The "Firework" fart (loud but odorless and dry)	*La pétarade*
The creaky door fart (a long, thin whistler)	*La Louise**

*("une LooooooouulllllZzeeuh") The biggest selling indie rock band of all-time in France was called "Louise Attaque"

A **burp**
*un **rot***

To **burp**
roter

Did your girlfriend
just **belch**?
*C'est ta copine qu'a
rote?*

A **fart**
*Un **pet***

To have **gas**
*Avoir des **gaz***

Who farted?
Qui c'est qui a pété?

Pierre **ripped one.**
*Pierre a **lâché une caisse**.*

Someone **dropped an atomic bomb.**
*Y'en a un qui a **lâché une bombe atomique**.*

That's not **my smell.**
*C'est pas **mon odeur**.*

You know how farts sometimes just slide right out? Well,
the French use this phenomenon to describe anything that
slides:

To slip or slide out like **a fart on wax paper**
*Glisser comme **un pet sur une toile cirée***

To slip or slide out like **a nun's fart against a stained
glass window**
*Glisser comme **un pet de bonne sœur sur le vitrail d'une
cathédrale***

·····Pissing
Pisser

In France, instead of "pissing in the wind" you "piss in a
violin" *(pisser dans un violon)*. And if you don't give a shit

about somebody, you say that you "piss on the part in their hair" *(pisser à la raie)*.

I gotta...
Je dois...

> **take a leak**
> *faire la vidange*
>
> **take a piss**
> *pisser*
>
> **tinkle**
> *faire pipi*

I gotta pee like a racehorse.
J'ai une putain d'envie de pisser.

I peed my pants.
Je me suis pissé dessous.

My brother's a **bedwetter**.
*Mon frère est une **pisseuse**.*

CHAPTER 5

HORNY FRENCH
LE FRANÇAIS BANDANT

The French have the reputation of being amazing lovers. Fact is, they're no physically better equipped to have sex than the rest of us. They just have more of it. Between their cushy 35-hour workweeks and five weeks of vacation a year, they simply have more time to fuck. Throw in their wine-fueled libertinism, and it's a minor miracle France doesn't have a population the size of China's.

·····Fucking
La baise

Tonight, I wanna…
Ce soir, je veux…

Let's go…
Allons…

You make me want to…
Tu me donnes envie de…

make love
faire l'amour

sleep with you
coucher avec toi
Literally, "bed you;" *dormir avec* — "sleep with" — means just that in French: catchin' Zs

fuck
baiser; piner

get off
tirer un coup
Literally, "To take a shot"

screw
niquer; tringler; troncher

fornicate
forniquer

get my rocks off
prendre mon pied
Literally, "to take my foot"

put it in your box
enfourner mon pain
Literally, "put my baguette in the oven"

ram you hard
te ramoner grave

fill you up
te bourrer

do the beast with two backs
faire la bête à deux dos

pound your ass
t'exploser la rondelle

fuck up the ass
enculer

fuck like rabbits
baiser comme des lapins

have a quickie
tirer un coup rapidos

do it woman on top
s'empaler la foufoune
Literally, "impale the muff"

·····Positions, etc.
(Les positions, etc.)

If you want to learn the best and most innovative positions ever made in France, check out skin flicks starring these Gallic porn superstars: Laure Sainclair, Katsumi, Clara Morgane, and the studs Sébastian Barrio and HPG (Henri-Pierre Gustave), the latter claiming measurements of 20 cms, which is metric for "huge."

Let's do…
Faisons…

Wanna try…?
Veux-tu essayer…?

How 'bout…?
Et si on faisait… ?

I'm tired of…
J'en ai marre de…

> **missionary style**
> *la position du missionnaire*
>
> **doggy style**
> *l'amour en levrette*
>
> **double penetration**
> *la double pénétration*
>
> **anal sex**
> *le sexe anal*
>
> **threesome**
> *le ménage à trois*
>
> **foursome/fivesome/etc.**
> *le plan baise à quatre/cinq/etc.*
>
> **group sex**
> *la partouze*

Two to lift her, three to fill her. (You know, the old porn cliché where two men hold the woman aloft and three others fill the usual orifices?)
Deux qui la tiennent, trois qui la pinent.

Take me **from behind** and cum in my ass.
*Prends-moi **par derrière** et jouis dans mon cul.*

·····The family jewels
Les bijoux de famille

The French could fill a small dictionary with all their words
for genitals. Sort of stands to reason that you'll have a lot of
words for something when people are always talking about it.

Suck my...
Suce-moi le/la...

Play with my...
Joue avec mon/ma...

> **penis**
> *pénis*
>
> **dick**
> *bite*
>
> **tubesteak**
> *vier*
> Literally, "my eggplant"
>
> **dong**
> *chibre*
>
> **prick**
> *dard*

COCK PARTY)))

Dicks come—as it were—in all shapes and sizes.

A big dick	*Une grosse bite*
A tiny dick	*Une petite bite*
A limp dick	*Une bite molle*
A half-boner	*Un bande-mou*
Hung like a horse	*Monté comme un âne*

purple-headed monster
chauve à col roulé
Literally, baldy in a turtleneck—ever looked closely at an uncircumsized penis?

I really like your huge...
J'adore...géant(e).

Geneviève thinks your...is so cute.
Geneviève trouve....vraiment mignon(ne).

snake
ta queue; ta pine
In French, "tail"—*la queue*—means "dick." So don't say "get some tail" unless you're really jonesin' for cock.

erection
ton érection

wood
ton gourdin
Literally, "a cudgel"

rod
ta verge; ta trique

tool
ton engin

the head
ton gland

wiener
ta saucisse

pecker
ta quéquette; ton zob

wee-wee
ton zizi; ta zézette

weenie
ta zigounette

wang
ton zguègue; ton zboub
You probably don't know why it's called a "wang." We have no friggin' idea why the French call it *"un zguègue."*

Tickle my...
Chatouille-moi...

Gargle my…
Gargarise-moi…

Massage my…
Masse-moi…

Can I shave your…?
Je peux te raser…?

> **testicles**
> *les testicules*

> **balls**
> *les couilles*

> **nuts**
> *les bonbons*

> **scrotum**
> *le scrotum*

> **package**
> *le paquet*

> **nards, nads**
> *les roupettes; les roubignoles*

Is your **nutsack** always that droopy?
T'as toujours la ***bourse*** qui pend comme ça?

·····Boobs
Lolos

I love…
J'adore…

Pinch my…
Pince-moi…

Can I squeeze your…?
Je peux te tripoter…?

> **tits**
> *les nichons; les nénés*

> **breasts**
> *les seins*

hooters
les nibards

boobs
les lolos

titties
les tétés

big tits
les gros nichons

huge tits
les seins énormes

DiRTY SONGS)))

CHANSONS PAILLARDES

Here are a few classic dirty French songs to help you keep pace when everyone at the table has had a few too many.

Ah-ah Bali-Balo	**Aaaah, Bali-Balo**
Bali-Balo est un salaud	**Bali-Balo is an assho'**
Bali Balo dans son berceau	**Bali-Balo rockin' in his craa-dle**
Bandait déjà comme un taureau	**Bali-Balo, already hung like a bull**
Fils de putain lui dit sa mère	**Son-of-a-bitch said his ma**
Tu bandes déja plus que ton père	**You're already harder than your pa.**
Le curé de Camaret a les couilles qui pendent	**The priest's balls are a hanging mass**
Et quand il s'assoit dessus	**And when he sits down on 'em good**
Ca lui rentre dans le cul	**They get pushed up his ass—**
Il bande, il bande, il bande.	**He gets wood, he gets wood, he gets wood.**
Tiens Marie voilà 100 sous	**Mary, a hundred cents is all I've got,**
Prends-moi les, rends moi 3 francs	**Take 'em and give me back three**
Non monsieur c'est trop peu	**No sir, that's not enough for me**
Pour sucer un si gros nœud.	**To suck such a gigantic knot.**

Nice…!
Jolis…!

You have great…
Tu as des…magnifiques.

> **airbags**
> *air-bags*

> **torpedoes**
> *obus*

> **nipples**
> *mamelons*

> **nips**
> *tétons*

> **fake tits**
> *faux seins*

> **boob job**
> *nibards siliconés*

She's got **no breasts**.
*Elle a **pas de seins**.*

She's as **flat as an ironing board**.
*Elle est **plate comme une planche à repasser**.*

That's a huge rack!
Il y a du monde au balcon!
Literally, "there's a crowd on the balcony"

She's got the **high beams** on.
*Elle nous fait un appel de **phares**.*

•••••Pussy
La chatte

Go down on my…
Va t'occuper de mon…

Be gentle with my…
Vas-y doucement avec mon…

> **vagina**
> *vagin*

pussy
minou; minet

cunt
con (not nearly as harsh or vulgar as in English)

clitoris
clitoris

clit
clito; clitos

button
bouton

G-spot
point G

You have such a tight...
Ta...est vraiment étroite.

Your...is so wet.
Ta...est tellement mouillée.

I wanna finger your...
Je veux mettre le doigt dans ta...

pussy
chatte

snatch
motte

clam
moule

sweaty clam
moule qui suinte

slit
fente

vulva
vulve

Lick my...
Lèche-moi ...

Eat my...
Bouffe-moi...

muff
la touffe

bush
le gazon
Literally, "the lawn"

fur
la fourrure

hairy pussy
la chatte touffue; la moule à bissus
Literally, "the hairs in a mussel's crack"

shaved pussy
la chatte rasée

Let's go **muff-diving**.
Allons brouter du gazon.

I'm gonna **seriously stuff your pussy**.
Je vais t'en mettre plein la chatte.

I'm so horny, my **cunt is on fire**.
J'ai tellement envie, j'ai la moule en feu.

He always gets my **slit wet**.
Avec lui j'ai la moule qui mouille.

Bitch, go get your **cunt pried open**!
Va te faire ouvrir la moule, connasse!

Damn, girl, your **pussy lips** taste so good.
Putain que j'adore le goût de tes lèvres.

That video's got some seriously gaping pussy.
Qu'est-ce qu'elle baille sérieusement de la chatte dans cette vidéo.

·····Ass
Cul

Anal sex is not as taboo in France, so you'll hear a lot of daily expressions using *enculer* (to ass-fuck or sodomize), including our personal favorite, *enculer les mouches*, which literally means "to ass-fuck flies" but is used to describe someone who "nitpicks over ridiculously small details."

You got a big ole...
T'as un/une putain de gros(se)...

Can I put it in your...?
Je peux le mettre dans ta/ton...?

Stick your fingers in my...
Mets tes doigts dans ma/mon...

Stroke my...
Caresse-moi la/le...

> **ass**
> *cul*
>
> **booty**
> *croupe*
>
> **asshole**
> *trou du cul*
>
> **buttcrack**
> *raie*
>
> **crack**
> *sourire vertical*
> Literally, "the vertical smile"
>
> **bunghole**
> *rondelle*

SEX RHYMES)))

The French are fond of making up little sex rhymes. The rhymes below aren't exactly up to Ludacris's standards, but they're still pretty fun in a dorky sort of way.

> **Women in glasses are crazy 'bout asses.**
> *Femme à lunettes, femme à quéquettes.*
> Literally, "lady in glasses is crazy for dick"
>
> **Girls named Toni like it boney.**
> *Martine, aime la pine.*
>
> **Balls, Mrs. Rawls—your dog screws mine, and you say it's fine?**
> *Mon vier Mme Olivier, votre chien encule le mien et vous dites que c'est rien?*

anus
anus

derriere
derrière

You have nice, strong **buttocks**.
*T'as des **miches** bien fermes et musclées.*

I want to lick you from your **hips** to your toes.
*Je veux te lécher des **hanches** jusqu'aux pieds.*

Let's **assfuck without lubricant**.
Enculons-nous à sec.

·····Sex Fluids and Pubic Hair
Les liquides et les poils de l'amour

Gross! I'm covered in…
Beurk! Je suis couvert de…

I've never seen so much/so many…in my life.
J'ai jamais vu tant de…de ma vie.

Can I eat/drink your…?
Je peux bouffer/boire ton/ta…?

cum
foutre

semen
sémence

sperm
sperme

pussy juice
crème de ta frambroise
Literally, "cream off your raspberry"

female ejaculation
éjaculation féminine

smegma
smegma

dickcheese
fromage de bite

short and curlies
foufoune; foufe

Shave my pussy.
Rase-moi la chatte.

I like to floss with **pubic hair**.
*J'aime me servir de **poils pubiens** comme fil dentaire.*

Your **pubes** are like steel wool.
*Tes **poils** on dirait de la laine de verre.*

Smear your **period blood** on me.
*Inonde-moi de tes **menstrues**.*

Shit on my chest.
***Chie-moi sur** la poitrine.*

Fuck me **in the shit**.
*Encule-moi **dans la merde**.*

When the river runs red, take the **Hershey trail**.
*Quand la rivière coule rouge, prends le **chemin boueux**.*
Literally, "the mud trail"

·····Foreplay
Les préliminaires

Sometimes it's not all about sex. Sometimes you gotta whisper a few sweet nothings into your lover's ear, give a little massage, and stop thinking about your own genitals for two seconds.

Can I...?
Je peux...?

> **kiss you**
> *t'embrasser*

> **suck you**
> *te sucer*

> **swallow you**
> *t'avaler*

I'm tired of...
Je suis fatigué(e) de...

French-kissing
rouler des pelles

hugging
faire des câlins

massaging your back
te masser le dos

trying to undo your fly
essayer d'ouvrir ta braguette

dry-humping
jouer à frotti-frotta
Literally, "playing rub-a-dub-dub"

finger-fucking
te doigter

burning rubber (fucking dry)
limer à sec

Have you ever…?
As-tu déjà…?

been in an orgy
participé à une orgie

organized a free-for-all
organisé une partouze

been sandwiched
pris en sandwich

done a skin flick
tourné dans un film de cul

SEX PROS)))

LES PROS DU SEXE

a prostitute	*une prostituée*
a streetwalker	*une péripatéticienne*
a whore	*une putain; une pute; poufiasse*
a dirty whore	*sale pute*
a pimp	*un maquereau; un mac*
a gigolo	*un gigolo*

Do it.../ I want it...
Fais-le.../Je le veux...

> **faster**
> *plus vite*

> **slower**
> *moins vite*

> **harder**
> *plus fort*

> **softer**
> *moins fort*

> **again**
> *encore*

> **again**
> *encore*

> **again**
> *encore*

•••••So You Don't Get Bored
Pour ne pas s'ennuyer

You know the old baseball analogy where first base means making out and a home run is sex? In the U.S., a lot of people will hand out the first few bases like free candy, but hold on to the home run ball for someone special. It's a little different in France. There, you're more likely to have sex than get a blow job or be eaten out, since oral sex is reserved for only the most intimate of couples. And swallowing after oral sex is even rarer still, because French girls *really* don't go for that.

> I **suck** but I don't **swallow**.
> *Je **suce** mais j'**avale** pas.*
> This is a pretty common way for French girls to announce the rules.
> Absolutely a classic.

> Can I **sit on your face**?
> *Puis-je **poser mon cul sur ta gueule**?*

How 'bout I **play the skin flute**?
*Je te **taille une pipe**?*
Literally, "whittling a wood pipe"

How 'bout a/some…?
Ça te dit…?

Have you ever tried…?
T'as déjà essayé…?

Let's switch it up and try…
Changeons un peu et essayons…

Let's film ourselves doing…
Filmons-nous en train de faire…

> **fellatio**
> *une fellation*
>
> **blowjob**
> *une turlute; un pompier; une pipe*
>
> **deep throat**
> *une gorge profonde*
>
> **cunnilingus**
> *le cunnilingus*
>
> **rim job**
> *la feuille de rose*
> Literally, "the pink leaf"
>
> **69**
> *le soixante-neuf*

MULTIPLE ORGASMS)))

I'm gonna...	Je vais...
orgasm	*jouir*
ejaculate	*éjaculer*
shoot my load	*lâcher la marchandise*
blow my wad	*envoyer la purée*
bust my nut	*balancer la sauce*
squirt	*gicler*
let go	*décharger*

titty-fucking
la branlette espagnole
Literally, "a Spanish hand job"

bondage/S&M
le bondage/S&M

anal penetration
la pénétration anale

sodomy
la sodomie

enema
un lavement

facial
l'éjac' faciale

> A bit of sage advice for men from the French philosophical tradition:
>
> **When everything's going wrong, treat yourself to a facial.**
> *Quand tout va mal, éjac' faciale.*

·····I'm coming!
Je jouis!

Grab some rubbers and memorize this section, because the only thing worse than not having a condom when you want to screw would be having to thumb through this chapter in the heat of the moment just to figure out how to tell your lover "*Je jouis! Je jouis! Je jouis!*"

I really like that!
J'aime beaucoup ça!

That's great!
C'est vraiment bon!

Are you getting hot?
Ça t'excite?

I'm totally drenched.
Je mouille comme une folle.
"I'm as wet as a crazy lady."

Damn, girl, I'm **getting hard.**
Oh putain, je commence à bander.

Do you have a **condom**?
Tu as un préservatif?

I want **to cum**.
Je veux jouir.

I'm about to cum.
Je suis sur le point de jouir.

I'm coming!
Je jouis!

Oh shit! I **busted the rubber**.
Merde! J'ai explosé la capote.
"Le capot" is the hood of a car, i.e., it covers the engine.

Can I cum…?
Je peux jouir…?

> **in your mouth**
> *dans ta bouche*
>
> **in your ass**
> *dans ton cul*
>
> **in your hand**
> *dans ta main*
>
> **on your face**
> *sur ton visage*
>
> **on your tits**
> *sur tes nichons*

Do you **masturbate**?
Tu te masturbes?

I **jack off** twice a day.
Je me branle deux fois par jour.

Go milk your rod.
Va faire pleurer le colosse.
Literally, "go make the giant cry"

Last night I had a **wet dream**.
*Hier soir j'ai eu une **émission nocturne**.*

Premature ejaculation is a bitch.
***L'éjaculation précoce** me casse les couilles.*

Fuck me with the **dildo**.
*Prends-moi avec un **godemichet**; un **gode**.*

Do you have a **vibrator**?
*Tu as un **vibromasseur**; un **vibro**?*

That girl'd **eat dick raw** if she could.
*Elle est bonne à **bouffer de la bite crue**.*

He/She is down to fuck.
Il/Elle a le feu au cul.

She loves the dick.
Elle est un cul à bites.
Literally, "she has an ass for dicks"

·····Sex fiends
Obsédé(e)s sexuels

Some people are defined by their job. Fluffers, for instance, are hired crew members whose job it is to keep male porn stars erect while they're off-camera getting ready for the next gang bang. Though you might not suck porn star dick for a living (not that there's anything wrong with that), chances are you've been defined by your sex life at one time or another.

My French boyfriend is...
Mon copain français est...

My American girlfriend is...
Ma copine américaine est...

Your ex sounds like...
Ton ex a l'air d'être...

Your mom is...
Ta mère est...

a sex fiend
un(e) obsédé(e) sexuel(le)

a nymphomaniac
une nymphomane

a horndog
un queuetard

a slut
une salope

a skank
une grognasse

a walking sperm bank
un garage à bites
Literally, "a parking garage for dicks"

a good fuck
un bon coup

a lousy lay
un mauvais coup

a virgin
une vierge; un puceau;
une pucelle

a sadist
sadique

a masochist
masochiste

sado-masochist
un sado-maso

a homo
homo

a fag
un pédé

a twinky
une pédale

a lesbian
lesbienne

a dyke
gouine; gazon maudit
Literally, "a lawn with a hex on it"

If she's gonna **lie there like a dead fish**, she's sleeping in the wet spot tonight.
*Si elle va rester là à **faire l'étoile de mer** normal qu'elle se tape la tache mouillée.*
Instead of "dead fish," the French say "starfish" because starfish have spread-open legs and never move.

·····Bad Shit
Des trucs tordus

French is the language of love and poetry, of passion and romance. An exceptionally lyrical language, it is intellectual and existential, sensual and sensitive, as evidenced in these genteel phrases.

That whore gave me...
Cette pute m'a donné/m'a filé...

That asshole gave me...
Cet enculé m'a donné/m'a filé...

> **crabs**
> *les morpions*

> **herpes**
> *l' herpès*

> **AIDS**
> *le SIDA (le syndrome d'immunodéficience acquise)*

> **HIV**
> *le VIH (le virus de l'immunodéficience humaine)*

> **an STD**
> *une MST (une maladie sexuellement transmisse)*

It's the first time I've had...
C'est la première fois que j'ai ...

> **blue balls**
> *des couilles molles*

numb dick
la bite engourdie

drippy dick
le robinet qui coule

raw vag
la chatte déchiquetée

It burns when I pee.
Ça brûle quand je pisse.

Do you have a pussy discharge?
Est-ce que ça suinte du pus?

CHAPTER 6

ANGRY FRENCH
LE FRANÇAIS DE LA COLÈRE

·····Pissed off
Pétage de plombs

Remember the World Cup, when Zidane head-butted that Italian sissy for calling his sister a whore? That was awesome! And not very representative of French culture. Your typical Frenchman will usually pose like a badass and make a lot of noise, but never actually throw down (just like your average rapper). This truism falls flat, though, when you enter the French ghettos on the outskirts of major cities, where about 100 cars are set on fire every weekend. So if you're into self-mutilation and internal bleeding, check it out! For the rest of us, there's deep breathing, counting to 10, and talking about our feelings.

Skinny French people...
Des Français maigrichons...

Fat tourists...
Des gros porcs de touristes...

Euro hipsters…
Les bobos…

> **are too much**
> *me gavent*

> **get on my nerves**
> *m'énervent*

> **get up my ass**
> *m'emmerdent*

> **tick me off**
> *me gonflent*

> **wear me out**
> *me saoulent*

> **think they're the shit**
> *se prennent pour le trou du cul de la planète*
> Literally, "the planet's bunghole"

> **think they're the center of the universe**
> *se prennent pour le centre du monde*

> **don't give a shit** about anybody else
> *s'en foutent des autres*

I can't…
Je peux pas…

> **stand you**
> *te supporter*

> **put up with them anymore**
> *les encadrer*

> **stand the sight of him/her**
> *le/la voir*

You are…
Tu es…

> **so full of shit**
> *complètement faux cul*

> **out of control**
> *complètement givré(e)*

> **a pain in the ass**
> *chiant(e)*

wacked out
cinglé(e); fêlé(e)

He/She...
Il/Elle...

looks like a real asshole
a une vraie tête de con

doesn't do a thing for me
a une tronche qui ne me revient pas

is bad news
a mauvais caractère

looks pissed
a l'air fou furieux

could kill you with one look
a des couteaux à la place des yeux

knifed me in the back
m'a poignardé dans le dos

stood me up
m'a posé un lapin
Literally, "left me a rabbit"

Stop...
Arrête...

busting our balls
de nous casser les couilles

sayin' shit about me
*de **raconter des saloperies** sur mon compte*

talkin' smack **behind my back**
*de raconter des trucs **dans mon dos***

lying like a rug
*de **mentir** comme tu respires*
Literally, "lying like you breathe"

·····Assholes
Enculé(e)s

Thanks to globalization, certain types of people now suck all over the world.

Boss
Le patron; le chef

> **My boss** is a first-rate asshole.
> ***Mon chef*** *est un enculé de première.*

My ex
Mon ex

> **My ex-boyfriend** was a cheap-ass.
> ***Mon ex*** *était un gros radin.*

> **My ex-girlfriend** was a frigid bitch.
> ***Mon ex*** *était une salope frigide.*

> **Your ex-husband** was kind of a sex freak, no?
> ***Ton ex*** *était un peu obsédé sexuel, non?*

Lawyer
Un(e) avocat(e)

> If you gave the Sahara to **a lawyer**, 10 years later
> you'd be out of sand!
> *Si tu donnes le Sahara à **un avocat**, dans 10 ans il faut
> acheter du sable ailleurs!*
> A famous joke from the beloved French comic Coluche

Politician
Un homme/une femme politique

> Never go with **a politician** into an airport bathroom.
> *Ne va jamais dans les chiottes de l'aéroport avec **un
> homme politique**.*

Telemarketer
Un télémarketeur/une télémarketeuse

> Is there anything more annoying than **a telemarketer**?
> *Y a rien de plus énervant qu'**un télémarketeur**!*

Stepmom
Belle-mère

> **My stepmom** totally confiscated my bong.
> ***Ma belle-mère*** *m'a confisqué la pipe à eau.*

Father-in-law
Beau-père

> **Your father-in-law** is kind of hard-ass, isn't he?
> ***Ton beau-père***, *c'est pas un peu un dur à cuire?*

Hipster
Un/une branché(e)

I hate **hipsters** and their Save the Planet bikes.
*Je peux pas les blairer ces **branchés** Vel' Lib'.*

Jock
Un sportif/une sportive

If the **jocks** at my school were any dumber, they'd be brain-dead.
*Plus cons que les **sportifs** de ma fac, tu meurs.*
"Any dumber than the jocks at my school and you wouldn't be breathing."

He's/She's a...
C'est un/une...

> **bastard**
> *connard/connasse*
>
> **tough customer**
> *un loubard*
>
> **thug**
> *voyou*
>
> **asshole**
> *salaud*
>
> **bitch**
> *salope; chienne*
>
> **skanky slut**
> *grosse pouffiasse*
>
> **motherfucker**
> *enculé(e)*
> Literally, "ass-fucked"
>
> **jerk**
> *enfoiré(e)*
>
> **loser**
> *cake*
>
> **dickhead**
> *tête de vier*

•••••The man with the badge
Les forces de l'ordre

On the list of people who are always there when you don't need them, cops deserve a special place. The French have a regular police force (*La police*) just like in the U.S. But they also have the *gendarmes*, a national police squad used mostly in the countryside who are a bit like the hick cops in old *Starsky and Hutch* episodes. And then there's the CRS, the riot police, a combination of national guard and SWAT team—these are the real badasses. When the shit goes down in Paris, the government sends out busloads of these guys packing helmets, masks, shoulder and knee pads, boots, batons, shields, and tear gas, like something straight out of *Blade Runner* or *Judge Dredd*. Use one of the following phrases right before they blast you in the face with pepper spray.

Watch out, here come **the cops**!
*Vingt-deux, v'là **les flics**.*
There are lots of explanations for the "vingt-deux" (22) but no one knows for sure.

Fucking cops.
Enculés de flics.

The men in blue
Les petits hommes bleus

The narcs
La brigade des stups
Short for *stupéfiants*, "stupefying," in the sense of intoxicating

The police wagon
Le panier à salade
"The salad basket," from the boxes used to ship heads of lettuce

The pigs
Les poulets
In France, cops are derogatorily called chickens rather than pigs.

Let's go. **Smells like bacon** around here.
*On se casse. **Ça sent la volaille** par ici.*

A motorcycle cop
Un motard

Look at 'em, all dressed up **on their bikes**. They look like the Village People!
*Regarde-les tout fiers **sur leurs motos**, on dirait les Village People!*

A K9 cop
Un maître chien

The **dog** is taking his cop for a walk.
*C'est le **chien** qui le tient en laisse.*

A meter maid
Un pigeon
Because of the snazzy powder-blue hat and pantsuit they wear

Why don't you **arrest** some real criminals instead of sticking me with **a parking ticket**?
*Vous feriez mieux **d'arrêter** de vrais criminels au lieu de me coller **un PV**!*

Watch it, this town is **full of speed traps**!
*Faites gaffe, ce bled est **bourré de radars**!*

No shit! **These clowns** think they're Starsky and Hutch!
***Ces enfoirés** se la jouent trop Starsky et Hutch, sans déconner!*

Fuck the police!
Nique la police!

·····Getting arrested
Se faire tauler

Remember, snitches get stitches. So if the pigs pick you up, you didn't see shit. Ya heard?

I won't say a word without my lawyer.
***Je dirais rien** sans un avocat.*

It wasn't me.
C'est pas moi.

I don't know anything.
Je sais rien.

Act like you don't know shit.
__Fais comme si__ de rien n'était.

Snitches get stitches.
Délater, tu te fais latter.

·····Fighting words
Ça va filer

To get a sense of how violent some of the bad neighborhoods in France are, rent *La Haine* (Hate) by Mathieu Kassovitz, France's answer to Quentin Tarantino. It takes place in the housing projects and starts with awesome battle scenes between the project dwellers and the CRS. After you get all juiced up on adrenaline, master the following phrases, grab your brass knuckles, and join in the fray.

I hate you.
Je te déteste.

Get lost.
Fous le camp.

Scram.
Dégage.

Go to hell.
Va te faire voir.

Leave me the hell alone.
Fous-moi la paix.

Fuck off.
Va te faire foutre.
Literally, "go make yourself come"

You're so **lame** at Gameboy!
T'es __une vraie quiche__ aux jeux vidéo!

He's a total **bummer.**
Il est complètement __nase__.

Chicken shit!
Couille molle!
Literally, "soft in the balls"

•••••More shit-talk
Toujours grande gueule

Most French shit talking isn't that different from what we say in the U.S. when we're fed up with someone's bullshit.

What did you just **say**!?!
*Qu'est-ce t'as **dit** là!?!*

You wanna **say that again**?
Répète un peu pour voir?

Shut your face.
Ferme ta gueule.; Ferme-la.

Shut the fuck up.
Ferme ta clape-merde.
Literally, "shut your shitmouth"

You're **worthless**.
*T'es un **moins que rien**.*

You got a **problem**?
*T'as un **problème**?*

Watch your ass!
Gare ta gueule!

Let's take it **outside**.
*Je t'attends **dehors**.*

I'll fix your ass.
Je vais te mettre ton compte.; Je vais te régler ton compte.

I'll have your **hide**.
*J'aurai ta **peau**.*

I got in a fight **last night**.
*Je me suis battu **hier soir**.*

Damn, they pounded the shit out of each other!
Putain, qu'est-ce qu'ils se sont mis!

They're gonna **throw down**.
Ça va filer!

Are there a lot of **bar brawls** in France?
*Est-ce qu'il y a beaucoup de **filades dans les bars** en France?*

·····Punches and kicks
Coups de poings et coups de pieds

To punch somebody
Frapper quelqu'un

To slap somebody
Gifler quelqu'un

To smack somebody
Donner une baffe à quelqu'un

To kick someone in…
Mettre un coup de pied dans…

> **the head**
> *la tête*

> **the stomach**
> *le ventre*

> **the butt**
> *le cul*

> **the balls**
> *les couilles*

To pound with your **fist**
Mettre un coup de poing

To **head-butt**
*Donner un **coup de tête/coup de boule***
"Coupe de boule" means to hit with the "bowling ball"

A bloody **nose**
*Saigner du **nez***

A black **eye**
*Un **œil** au beurre noir*
Literally, "an eye with black butter"

He **busted** that guy's nose.
*Il lui a **cassé** le nez au mec.*

Yo! **Mudwrestling**, I'm all over that!
*Oh! **Les combats dans la boue**, j'adore ça!*

·····The art of the French insult
L'art de l'insulte à la française

The word *con* is used to say just about everything in French slang. It comes from the same word as "cunt," but doesn't have that word's harshness. It's much closer to "jerk" or "ass." The French combine it with various adjectives to give it different meanings.

Un con
An ass

Un pauvre con
A pathetic loser

Un petit con
A sneaky jerk

Un gros con
A screaming asshole

Un brave con
A loser with a good heart

France isn't nearly as PC as the U.S., so race talk gets people riled up but not as much as it does in the States.

Fuck your race.
Nique ta race.

Typical ethnic bastard.
Enculé de ta race.
Literally means "assfuck of your race" but loosely translates to
"you're just like every other white/black/Latino/…bastard"

Instead of race, anything with "mother" in it is gonna get French dudes really pissed off. It's a Catholic country, goddammit! What the motherfuck do you expect?

Motherfucker
Enculé de ta mère

Fuck your mother.
Nique ta mère.

Your mother's a whore.
Ta mère la pute.

Son-of-a-bitch
Fils de pute

Your mother **gave birth in a trash can**.
*Ta mère elle **a accouché dans une poubelle**.*
A classic French middle school insult

They also have the French equivalent of our old "Your mother wears army boots," which will often just make people laugh.

Your momma works at Sam's Club.
Ta mère elle travaille à Monoprix.
Monoprix is the French equivalent of the U.S. superstore.

Yeah, well, your momma wears a thong on TV.
Ta mère en string à la télé.

·····The peacemaker
Le pacifiste

Mellowed out, Owen Wilson surfer types *do* exist in the southwest of France. On the Mediterranean coast they're more into windsurfing (*planche à voile*) and energy drinks, while out in the countryside they're pot-smoking vegetarians who gave up their Mercedes in the city to commune with nature. But deep down inside, they all want everyone to just get along.

Yo, **dude**, it's all right, **chill out**.
*Ça va, **mec**, c'est bon, **calme-toi**.*

No need to get **all worked up**.
*Faut pas **t'exciter** comme ça.*

Don't get yourself in **such a state**.
*Faut pas te mettre dans **des états pareils**.*

That doesn't help a thing.
Ça sert à rien.

What got into you?
Qu'est-ce qui t'as pris?

Take a **deep breath**.
*Respire un **bon coup**.*

I'm **laid back**.
*Je suis un **calme**.*

I don't like getting **involved**.
*J'aime pas les **embrouilles**.*

Forget about it.
Laisse tomber; laisse béton.

Get over it.
Tourne la page.

Who gives a shit!?
Qu'est-ce qu'on s'en bat les couilles!?

Knock it off.
Arrête tes conneries.

Call **an ambulance**.
*Appelle **le SAMU**. (Service d'Aide Médicale Urgente)*

Call **the cops**.
*Appelle **les flics**.*

CHAPTER 7

POPPY FRENCH
LA CULTURE POP FRANÇAISE

·····Movies
Le cinéma

France has the third-largest film industry in the world (behind India and the U.S.). But if it weren't for France we wouldn't even *have* movies, since it was two French brothers, Auguste and Louis Lumière, who invented the film camera. A lot of French movie genres parallel the English: *un film d'action, un film d'horreur, un film romantique, un film de science fiction,* and so on. If you hate *les comédies musicales* as much as we do, you can always lie to your friends and claim this book says they don't exist in France.

Wanna catch **a movie**?
*On se regarde **un film**?*

Wanna go see **a flick**?
*On va au **cinoche**?*

How 'bout a...?
Ça te dirait...?

cartoon
un dessin animé

tearjerker
un film à l'eau de rose

grandma movie
un film cucul la praline

chick flick
un film pour les gonzesses

dubbed movie
un film doublé; un film en v.f. (en version française)
Except in Paris, foreign films in theaters and on TV are usually dubbed

AMERICAN CLASSICS, FRENCH STYLE)))

In France, American films sometimes keep their original English titles and sometimes get totally new ones.

Meet the Parents	*Mon Beau-père et moi* My father-in-law and me
Something About Mary	*Mary à tout Prix* Mary at any cost
Jaws	*Les Dents de la mer* The teeth of the sea
Good Fellas	*Les Affranchis* The liberated
Shawshank Redemption	*Les Évadés* The escapees
Die Hard	*Piège de Cristal* The crystal trap
Deer Hunter	*Voyage au Bout de l'enfer* Journey to the end of Hell
The Bourne Ultimatum	*La Vengeance dans la peau* Vengeance in my blood
Groundhog Day	*Un Jour sans fin* The endless day
The Departed	*Les Infiltrés* The infiltrators

movie with subtitles
un film en v.o. (en version originale)
i.e., in its original language with subtitles

skin flick
un film de cul

Dude! They show **porn** on French TV!
*Hé mec! Ils passent des **films de cul** à la télé française!*

I'm tired of these **lame-ass movies**.
*J'en ai marre de ces **films bouffe-couilles**.*
Literally, "movies that eat your balls"

Let's see it on the **big screen**.
*On se le mate sur **grand écran**.*

Get me **a ticket**.
*Donnez-moi **une place**.*

Hey! **The line** starts back there!
*Oh! **La queue** c'est là-bas derrière qu'elle commence!*

Stallone sounds stupid even when he's **dubbed**!
*Stallone a l'air abruti même **en v.f.**!*

Kick the back of my chair one more time and I'll stuff that
popcorn through your face.
*Tu me mets encore un coup de pied dans le fauteuil et les
pop-corn je te les rentre par le nez!*

•••••Comics
La BD

Graphic novels are considered an art form and have an
illustrious history in France. In any French bookstore, you'll
find a comics section where adults and kids alike sit and
read for hours. Classic French comic heroes include the
accident-prone *Gaston Lagaffe*, the seafaring adventurer
Corto Maltese, and the quick-drawing cowboy *Lucky Luke*
who "shoots faster than his shadow." Currently, *The Nikopol
Trilogy* is popularizing futurist comics, while *Filthy Disgusting
Bastard* brings hard-core humor to the masses.

Do you have any…?
Avez-vous…?

>**comic books**
>*des bandes dessinées*

>**comics**
>*des BD*

>**new editions**
>*des nouvelles éditions*

>**first editions**
>*des premières éditions*

Who's your favorite…?
Qui est ton…?

>**superhero**
>*super héros favori*

>**villain**
>*méchant préféré*

>**sidekick**
>*frère d'armes préféré*

>**mutant**
>*mutant favori*

>**monster**
>*monstre préféré*

>**nefarious evildoer**
>*scélérat néfaste favori*

Some of the classics:

>***Les Aventures de Tintin et Milou***
>The Adventures of Tintin and Milou
>Written and drawn by the Belgian Hergé, this is probably the most famous French-language comic of all time. It tells of Tintin, a young reporter, and his dog Milou who travel around the world and even to the moon to solve mysteries.

>***Les Aventures d'Astérix le Gaulois***
>Asterix
>A close second in international popularity is *Asterix the Gaul*, written by René Goscinny and drawn by the Belgian

Albert Uderzo. These patriotic tales tell the story of a small Gallic village in Brittany, led by the mustachioed hero Asterix, that resists the Roman Invasion thanks to powers acquired by drinking a magical potion. Asterix was no surrender monkey!

Le Petit Nicolas
Little Nicholas

These hugely popular kids' stories, originally published in the early '60s, were also written by René Goscinny and were illustrated by Jean-Jacques Sempé, from the perspective of Little Nicholas himself and showing his child's-eye view of the world. His naïve perceptions often reveal themselves to be truer than those of the adults around him.

·····Music
La musique

Didja know that France is the second-largest market for rap in the world, behind the U.S.? Or that the Stade de France soccer stadium outside Paris is one of the biggest concert venues in Europe? Or that most French people don't give a damn about country music? Or that Air France's music channels suck? Now you do!

I'm with the **band**.
*Je fais partie du **groupe**.*

BY ANY OTHER NAME)))

Most styles of current music come from the U.S., so the names are the same in French: *le rock, le rap, le hip-hop, le funk, la soul, le R 'n' B, la disco, la techno, l'électro, la country, le jazz, la musique classique, le reggae, le ska, la world*. Exceptions: *La variété* is code for "Céline Dion Hell," and *la trad'* for the French version of alt-co (music from Britanny or Corsica, for instance, that uses regional instruments made from sheep guts and that are sung in indecipherable local dialects).

I'm totally into **rap**.
*Je kiffe grave le **rap**.*

I play my **tunes** *loud*!
*J'écoute la **'zique** à fond!*

I can't stand that…
Je peux pas supporter…

I'm in love with that…
J'adore…

>**musician**
>*ce/cette musicien(ne)*

>**lead singer**
>*ce chanteur/cette chanteuse*

>**drummer**
>*ce batteur*

>**bassist**
>*ce/cette bassiste*

>**guitar player**
>*ce/cette guitariste*

>**album**
>*ce disque*

>**song**
>*cette chanson*

>**cover song**
>*cette reprise*

>**encore**
>*ce rappel*

>**lyrics**
>*ce texte*

Where can we catch…?
Où peut-on écouter…?

>**some good tunes** around here
>*de la bonne **'zique** par ici*

>**some live music** in this town
>*de la **musique en direct** dans ce bled*

a good **concert**
*un bon **concert***

We're here **to record** our new album.
*On est ici pour **enregistrer** notre nouveau disque.*

Girl drummers are hot.
*Les **batteurs-filles** sont bandantes.*

My roommate **sings ABBA in the shower**.
*Mon camarade de chambre **chante ABBA dans la
douche.***

Crank it!
Monte le son!

·····Stars and superstars
Stars et superstars

The French *love* pop culture name-dropping. Learn the
following so that they won't ask if you're from Texas.

Gérard Depardieu
"Gégé" is the guy American directors get whenever they
need a French actor. He's probably appeared in every
single French movie that has played in the U.S. since
the '70s. He takes so many roles that he makes Kevin
Bacon look like a hermit: You could play Six Degrees of
Depardieu and never have to go past the second degree.
He's so well-known that his appearance is part of French
vocabulary:

> *Tu l'as vu celui-là, il a **le nez de Depardieu**.*
> Check that guy out, he's got a **Depardieu nose**.

Audrey Tautou
The adorable face of *Amélie*, she was chosen as the
French actress for *The Da Vinci Code*. French folks love
her or despise her. Check out *Baby Blues* if you want to
see her in a nude scene.

Gad Elmaleh, Djamel Debbouze, and Coluche
Three of the most popular stand-up comedians in France
who have crossed over to movies. Djamel was also

in *Amélie* and comes from the tough housing projects outside Paris. Coluche was France's John Belushi; he was so famous that he even ran for president before dying in a motorcycle accident in the mid-80s.

Jean Reno
You've probably seen him in a couple of Hollywood movies (*The Professional, Ronan, Mission Impossible*) as the surly badass with the ever-present five o'clock shadow. In France he's about as big as Bruce Willis.

Sophie Marceau
She was the hot French queen in *Braveheart*. On the red carpet at the Cannes Film Festival she pulled a Janet Jackson—one tit jumped out of her designer dress and became a viral hit on the Internet. Google "Sophie Marceau," "Cannes," and "tit" to witness history.

Johnny Hallyday
This guy is a major French icon. Ever since the early '60s he's been the most popular rock singer in the country. Imagine Elvis alive today, and that's what you'd have—a guy with so many face-lifts he gets mixed up with Joan Rivers. He uses a stage name because his real one, Jean-Philippe Smet, doesn't sound very rock 'n' roll.

MC Solaar, Suprême NTM, and IAM
These guys gave French rap some street cred in the late '80s and still call the shots today. With a degree in literature from the prestigious Sorbonne, Solaar creates texts and beats that are smoother and more poetic. IAM (from Marseille) and especially NTM (from around Paris) are closer to gangsta rap for style and politics; think Public Enemy and NWA, respectively. Joey Starr and Kool Shen, the founding members of NTM, have kept their reputation as the most controversial rappers around. Take their group's name, for starters: NTM stands for "*Nique ta mère*" or "Fuck your mother."

Unless you have a death wish, note the subtle difference between the following sentences:

> ***J'adore Nique Ta Mère*** (I love Fuck Your Mother)
> ***J'adore niquer ta mère*** (I love fucking your mother)

Noir Désir
In the '90s, Noir Désir was France's Nirvana, the greatest

and most popular alternative rock group in the country. Unfortunately, the Nirvana parallels didn't end there. In 2003 the band came to a dramatic end when lead singer Bertrand Cantat accidentally killed his girlfriend in a drunken rage. He was sentenced to prison for eight years and in 2007 was paroled.

Michel Drucker

The Dick Clark of France, he's been hosting TV shows since the '60s. A favorite of the geriatric generation, he's considered a has-been by everybody else—unless you happen to have a record or movie coming out, when a single appearance on his show is still a ticket to the big time. The best-known Drucker episode goes back to when he had Whitney Houston, at her peak, on his live show along with French singer (and notorious drunk) Serge Gainsbourg. Drucker pointed out that Gainsbourg's English was pretty good, and a wasted Gainsbourg turned to Whitney and said, "Yeah, and I want to fuck you!"

Zinédine Zidane

Playmaker for "Les Bleus" (the French national soccer team), Zidane led his country to its first-ever World Cup title, with two goals in the July 1998 final against Brazil. Alas, Zizou (as he's known in France) will be best remembered for head-butting Italian defender Marco Materazzi in overtime of the 2006 World Cup; France eventually lost in penalty kicks and it was the last game of Zidane's career. Zidane lost his cool on this exchange:

> **Zidane:** *Qu'est-ce que t'as à me tirer sur **le maillot** comme ça? **Si tu le veux**, je te le donne après le match.* (Why're you holdin' on to my **jersey** like that? **If you want it**, I'll give it to you after the game.)

> **Materazzi:** *Non, merci, je préfère **ta grosse pute de sœur**.* (No, thanks—I'd rather have **your nasty whore of a sister**.)

·····Gamers and techies
Joueurs et bidouilleurs

Some things are universal. French youth have joined the nerd fest. These days it's almost impossible to find an Internet café that isn't crammed with a bunch of zit-faced teenagers wearing headsets and screaming across the room that they just assfucked your module lander and power-boosted their Vorton shield to 3.5 mill' megavolts.

I'll kick your ass…
Je vais te mettre minable…

> **at video games**
> *aux jeux vidéo*

> **at Playstation**
> *à la Playstation*

> **on the computer**
> *à l'ordinateur*

> **at Guitar Hero**
> *sur Guitar Hero*

Don't touch…
Ne touche pas…

Press…
Appuie sur…

> **my control**
> *mon joystick*

> **the pause button**
> *le bouton de pause*

> **the trigger**
> *la gâchette*

> **the joystick**
> *le joystick*

You always press **reset** right when I'm about to destroy you.
*Tu appuies toujours sur le **bouton de remise à zero** quand je suis sur le point de te détruire.*

Download it to my…
Télécharge-le sur mon…

It's on my…
C'est sur mon…

laptop
portable
Cell phone; also laptop computer

iPod
iPod
Pronounced "EEE-pod"

MP3
mp3
"m-pay-twah"

Walkman
baladeur

CD player
lecteur CD

program
logiciel

USB key drive
clé USB

hard drive
disque dur

I blew out my hard drive.
J'ai explosé mon disque dur.

We downloaded **a shitload of MP3s.**
*On a téléchargé **toute une flopée de mp3.***

Send me an **e-mail**.
*Envoie-moi un **e-mail**/un **courriel**.*

Did you get my **text message?**
*T'as eu mon **texto**?*

There's no **Internet café** nearby?
*Y a pas un **cyber café** dans le coin?*

Do you have an American **keyboard?**
*Vous avez des **claviers** américains?*

·····Fashion
La mode

Fashion is another area where the French set the international standard. Many of the greatest designers and brands, past and present, come from France: Coco Chanel, Christian Dior, Pierre Cardin, Guess, Lacoste. While it may be cool in the U.S. to show up looking like you just dragged your ass out of bed, that shit won't fly in France.

I love your **outfit**!
*J'adore ta **tenue**!*

You've got a great **look**.
*J'adore ton **look**.*

I don't like her/his **walk**.
*J'aime pas sa **dégaine**.*

You're totally sexy **in that**.
*T'es super sexy **comme ça**.*

I can't believe he's wearing that!
Il est putain de mal fringué, je le crois pas!

You fucked up my **favorite shirt**!
*Tu m'as salopé ma **chemise préférée**!*

Go put on a/some...
Va te mettre un/une/des...

Take off that/those...
Enlève ce/cette/ces...

> **dirty clothes**
> *fringues dégueulasses*
>
> **dress clothes**
> *tenue de soirée*
>
> **tuxedo**
> *smoking*
>
> **evening gown**
> *robe de soirée*

suit
costard

pants
falzar

kicks (shoes)
godasses

sunglasses
lunettes de soleil

You planning on robbing a convenience store in that **ski mask**?
*Tu vas faire un casse dans une station service avec ta **cagoule**?*

Nice **threads**!
*Belles **fringues**!*

Oh shit! It's Bigfoot in a **thong**!
*On dirait Carlos **en string**!*

In that **suit**, you da' Man.
*T'es trop classe avec ton **costard**.*

You're lookin' all…
T'as l'air très…

   in fashion
   à la mode

THE LAST LAYER)))

LA DERNIÈRE ÉTOFFE

Tighty-whities	*Un slip*
Boxers	*Un caleçon*
Underwear	*Slip*
Bra	*Un soutien-gorge; un sous-tifs*
Panties	*Une culotte*
Thong	*Un string*
Speedo	*Un slip de bain*
Bikini	*Un bikini*

well-dressed
bien sapé(e)

badly dressed
mal sapé(e)

yuppie
BCBG (Bon Chic Bon Genre)

trendy
tendance

·····The Media
Les médias

From the press to the radio to TV shows, here's everything you need to know about French media.

NEWSPAPERS (*LES JOURNAUX*)
Since France is smaller than the U.S. (roughly the size of Texas), newspapers tend be national rather than regional. The four major papers are:

> *Le Monde:* No color pictures, no comics—just serious news.
> *Le Figaro:* The paper for wealthy conservatives.
>
> *Libération:* For hipsters and wannabes.
>
> *L'Equipe:* Like *The Sporting News* but daily!

While the first three are equivalent to *The New York Times* or *The Washington Post*, the fourth covers only sports and outsells all the others. They all struggle today, though, because of Internet news and because in Paris you can now get free newspapers at the métro.

MAGAZINES (*MAGAZINES*)
There are four weekly newsmagazines. *Paris Match* is a deliberate imitation of our former *Life Magazine*, while *Le Point, L'Express,* and *Le Nouvel Observateur* match up with our *Time, Newsweek,* and *U.S. News & World Report.*

To get the latest celeb news *(les infos people)* on who's sleeping with who, and to see pix of the latest nip slip, ask for *Gala, Voici,* or *VSD* (Fri.-Sat.-Sun.), the French equivalents of magazines like *People* and *Us Weekly*. This fascination with celebrity gossip has been a recent discovery for the French, who, for the longest time, thought they didn't like this kind of thing, but are now obsessed with it…. Sarkozy even got elected president by exploiting it.

Not everyone in France has discovered the Internet, so you can still find a couple of skin 'zines on news racks. *Lui* (For him), the French *Playboy*, and *Photo* are the most popular.

RADIO STATIONS (*STATIONS DE RADIO*)

In the early '90s, Brit pop and American music became so dominant that French bands couldn't even get on the radio anymore. The government intervened with a 1994 law forcing stations to dedicate at least 60 percent of prime-time airplay to French music. French R&B and rap artists have been the big beneficiaries of this new law. Here are some of the best-known French radio stations.

Turn it to…
Mets…

They play the worst music on…
Ils jouent la musique la plus nulle sur…

I only listen to…
Je n'écoute que…

NRJ (pronounced "N-R-G," a pun on "energy"): Pop music that teens like. A kind of MTV for radio.

Skyrock: R&B, rap, hip-hop, and some of the most outrageous shock jocks. Think Howard Stern introducing songs by Jay-Z.

Radio FG: Techno, electronica, R&B. The French home of Paul Oakenfold and ravers everywhere.

Radio Nostalgie: Retro French from the '70s. Some people just can't get over their glory days.

Rire et Chansons (Laughs and songs): An experimental format alternating between radio hits and stand-up comedy. It's a bizarre and strangely enjoyable combination; nothing like it in the U.S.

RMC Info: Talk radio, big on sports. Exactly like your average sports show in the U.S. except the host is named Luis instead of Mad Dog, and he spends most of his time yammering on about soccer.

Radio France: The French government has its own programming, divided into several different stations.

France Inter: News ("*Les Infos*") and talk radio; similar to the BBC.

France Culture: Highbrow radio on the arts; like those late-night segments on NPR that no one has ever actually listened to completely.

France Musique: Classical music and opera 24/7, but with one redeeming factor: All the DJs are women who sound like they trained on 900 numbers.

FRENCH TV (*LA TÉLÉ*)

You can't escape trashy American TV merely by coming to France. Most popular American shows, and even some American rejects, run dubbed in French. Now you know why they hate us.

Let's watch…
Regardons…

…is my favorite show
…est mon émission préférée

Is…on?
Est-ce que…passe maintenant?

American Idol
La Star Academy

Survivor
Koh Lanta

Wheel of Fortune
La Roue de la Fortune

The Price Is Right
Le Juste Prix

Not all French television is trashy, though. Here are some of the shows popular with "the crossword puzzle set" (that is, nerds and geezers):

Des Chiffres et des lettres
Numbers and Letters

An institution in France, it was created in the late '60s and is still going strong. In front of a live audience, a pair of candidates clash in two categories: come up with the longest word using nine randomly drawn letters; and cook up a math operation (adding, dividing, etc.) with a randomly selected series of numbers to arrive at a particular sum. If you're watching it for the first time, you'll wonder what the hell is going on—but these people are scary smart!

Questions Pour un Champion
Questions for a Champion

It's kind of like Jeopardy but in reverse. The host, Julien Lepers, looks as if he took some kind of energy drink or bumped a few lines of cocaine right before the show. He's massively popular with France's elderly population. Imagine Dick Clark fused with Bob Barker and you'll start to understand the geriatric powers he holds.

Histoires Naturelles
Nature Stories

When you get back from the club in the middle of the night and turn on the TV, you'll think you're hallucinating when you catch an episode of this boring shit. It's usually just endless shots of some guy walking in the forest with his dog, or sitting by a river listening to the sounds of the water and admiring the birds. Watch this for a few minutes and you'll start to think that bass-fishing infomercials are a real party.

CHAPTER 8

SPORTY FRENCH
LE FRANÇAIS SPORTIF

•••••The essentials
Les essentiels

Soccer is called "football" or just "foot" in France, and is far and away the most popular sport in the country. Nothing else even comes *close*. Women, however, don't play it and rarely watch it. Other big sports are tennis, rugby, bicycling, judo, skiing, and Formula One racing, which is like a less-hicked-out version of NASCAR.

I play...
Je joue au...

Do you play...?
Est-ce que tu joues au...?

Wanna go play some...?
Tu veux jouer au...?

Let's see if there's any...on TV.
Voyons voir s'il y a du.... à la télé.

> **soccer**
> *football; foot*

indoor soccer
foot en salle

tennis
tennis

golf
golf

basketball
basket

volleyball
volley

bowling
bowling (pronounced "BOO-ling")

football
football américain

baseball
baseball

hockey
hockey sur glace

rugby
rugby

bocce ball
aux boules; à la pétanque

I'm a **black belt** in judo.
*Je suis **ceinture noire** de judo.*

I can **break** three **bricks** with my hand.
*Je peux **casser** trois **briques** avec ma main.*

Bowling is a **sport** for jackoffs.
*Le bowling est un **sport** de branleurs.*

The **gold-medal winner** is built like an East German swimmer.
*La **médaille d'or**, elle a le physique d'une nageuse est-allemande.*

Zimbabwe's **national anthem** is that Monty Python song.
*L'**hymne national** du Zimbabwe c'est la chanson des Monty Python.*
No, seriously, the Monty Python theme song really is the Zimbabwe national anthem.

·····Live from the stadium
En direct du stade

If you get a chance to go to a soccer game in France, jump on it. The French national team plays in the Stade de France (in Saint-Denis, just north of Paris). The two most famous pro teams are Paris–St. Germain (PSG), whose home field is the Parc des Princes in southwest Paris, and Olympique de Marseille (OM), which does battle in the Stade Vélodrome down on the Mediterranean coast. The bitter rivalry between PSG and OM is similar to that of the Yankees and Red Sox—except that Red Sox fans don't fight it out with Yankees fans with bats and bricks at highway rest stops.

Let's go to…
Allons à…

a game
un match

a football game
un match de foot

a match
une partie

the championship game/the final
la finale

the tournament
un tournoi

the stadium
au stade

the field
sur le terrain

Check out…
Regarde…

the scoreboard
le tableau d'affichage

the players
les joueurs

OTHER SPORTS)))

Skiing is a huge sport in France, especially in the Alps. But be prepared for total anarchy at the ski lifts. Orderly lines don't exist in France (this is also true of airports, bar counters, ticket lines, and the like). Be ready to bull your way through, and don't hesitate to put your skis on top of someone else's. Also, it may be cool in the U.S. to walk around with your old lift tickets still clipped to your jacket, but in France you'll look like a dumbass. It's a ski resort, moron; of course you've hit the slopes.

The French are great at...	Les Français sont très forts...
skiing	au ski
biking	au vélo
jogging	au footing
skateboarding	au skate
waterskiing	au ski nautique
surfing	au surf
windsurfing	à la planche à voile
swimming	à la natation
gymnastics	à la gymnastique
track and field	à l'athlétisme
archery	au tir à l'arc
combat sports	aux sports de combat
martial arts	aux arts martiaux
boxing	à la boxe
judo	au judo
karate	au karaté
tae kwon do	au tae kwon do
wrestling	à la lutte
pro wrestling	au catch (fake WWE style)
ATB or MTB	au VTT ("vélo tout terrain")
mountain climbing	à l'alpinisme
rock climbing	à l'escalade
scuba diving	à la plongée
rafting	au rafting
sportfishing	à la pêche au gros
	Literally, "fishing for big ones"
skankfishing	à draguer les gros thons
	Literally, "fishing for nasty tuna," i.e., hitting on uglies

the teams
les équipes

Is it **halftime** yet?
*C'est bientôt la **mi-temps**?*

This **league** is stacked.
*Le **championnat** est franchement costaud.*

·····The fans
Les supporteurs

The U.S. believes in free enterprise, so heckling by the crowd is done on an individual basis. France believes in unions, so they have organized fan clubs in the stands, complete with microphones and memorized songs. Not only do they support the team by acting as the Twelfth Man and booing the opposing team—actually, they whistle in France—but they can even exert pressure in personnel decisions or force management to invest more money in the free-agent market. These people are rabid fanatics, even to the point of tragedy: Every year a few deaths occur in brawls between rival European clubs.

The stands
Les tribunes

The fans
Les supporteurs

To bet
Parier

The referee
L'arbitre

Fan clubs
Les clubs de supporteurs

Banner displays in the end zones
Les tifos

Where can I **watch** the game tonight?
*Où puis-je **voir** le match ce soir?*

Is the game **on the tube**?
*On donne le match **à la télé**?*

Who's playing?
C'est qui contre qui?

What's the **score**?
*Quel est le **score**?*

Who **scored**?
*Qui a **marqué**?*

Wanna get a cold one **at the half**?
*On se boit une mousse **à la mi-temps**?*
You'll only get to use this if you watch the game at someone's house or in a bar; no alky-hol allowed in French stadiums.

What an awesome **goal**!
*Quel **but** magnifique!*

That'll make the **highlight reel**!
*C'est un but **d'anthologie**!*

The **ref** robbed us!
*On s'est fait voler par **l'arbitre**!*

The ref is a **fucking asshole**.
*L'arbitre est un **gros enculé**.*

Our team's gonna **paste** you this year!
*Notre équipe va vous **laminer** cette année!*

We are the **champions**.
*On est les **champions**.*

•••••Board and bar games
Sports de salon et de troquet

Sometimes you just don't feel like running much. In addition to the grueling efforts required by armchair quarterbacking, these games go down easy with pizza and beer.

Do I look like someone who can do **crosswords**?
*J'ai une tête à faire des **mots croisés**?*

Every time you do **sudokus** in the car, you end up puking.
*À chaque fois que tu fais des **sudoku** en bagnole, tu finis par gerber.*

Did you do that Mickey Mouse **jigsaw puzzle** all by yourself?
*Tu l'as fait tout seul ce **puzzle** de Mickey Mouse?*

Does "shithead" count in **Scrabble**?
*On compte ou pas "tête de con" au **Scrabble**?*
Pronounced "SCRA-bleuh"

I play **strip poker** just to flash my tats and piercings.
*Je joue au **strip-poker** rien que pour faire mater mes tatouages et mes piercing.*

Let's play...
Jouons...

> **board games**
> *à des jeux de société*
>
> **Monopoly**
> *au Monopoly; au Monop'*
>
> **chess**
> *aux échecs*
>
> **checkers**
> *au jeu de dames*
>
> **cards**
> *aux cartes*
>
> **poker**
> *au poker*
>
> **rummy**
> *au rami*
>
> **bridge**
> *au bridge*

We suck at...
On est nulls au/aux...

> **pool**
> *billard*
>
> **darts**
> *fléchettes*

pinball
flipper

foosball
baby foot

•••••Hitting the weights
Se mettre aux haltères

You won't see many fat people in France. In fact, "obese" by French standards doesn't even qualify for "overweight" in U.S. statistics.

I do...
Je fais...

some exercise
de l'exercice

some lifting
de la muscu

some weightlifting
des haltères

stationary riding
du vélo de salon

push-ups
des pompes

aerobics
de l'aérobic

yoga
du yoga

The gym
Le gym

The weight room
La salle de muscu

The treadmill
Le tapis de course

The exercise mat
Le tapis de sol

The weights
Les haltères

I hit the **weight room** every day.
*Je vais à la **salle de muscu** tous les jours.*

Can I help?
Je peux vous aider?

Maybe we could **kick back** later **in the Jacuzzi**?
*On pourrait peut-être **se relaxer** après **dans le Jacuzzi**?*

Check out how **buff** he is.
*T'as vu comme il est **baraqué**.*

I got a ways to go before I get **washboard abs**.
*Pour les abdos, c'est pas encore des **tablettes de chocolat**.*
Literally, "chocolate bars"

·····The main events
Les grandes manifestations sportives

In France, March Madness comes when the European Soccer Champion's League reaches the direct elimination stages, and France's Superbowl is the Cup final in May. But the entire country eagerly awaits a bunch of other events.

The French Pro Soccer League
Le Championnat de France de Ligue 1
From August to May, 20 teams play each other twice (home and away). They get 3 points for a win, 1 for a tie, and nothing for a loss. (No penalty kick shoot-outs are allowed, except in finals and the French Open Cup.) At season's end, the last three teams drop in disgrace down

into the minor league and are replaced by the top three from the second division ("Ligue 2"). Because France imposes a luxury tax, stars like Thierry Henry, Patrick Vieira, and Franck Ribéry leave to play in the English, Italian, Spanish, or German leagues.

World Cup Soccer
La Coupe du Monde de football
It's *the* most-watched event on the planet. Americans think it's boring, but people in Brazil jump out of windows when the national team loses. Brazil has won the most titles (five), while France won it for the first and only time in 1998. In 2006 France lost in the finals to Italy in overtime after French superstar Zinédine Zidane was ejected from the game (the last of his career) for headbutting Italian defender Marco Materazzi for calling his sister a whore (see Chapter 7). It was a shocking end to an otherwise stellar career. Not quite as dramatic as the career-ending scene in *The Last Boy Scout* where the wide receiver is running up the field and is about to be tackled when all of a sudden he whips out a glock and starts pumping bullets into every defender…but still pretty dramatic.

The Olympic Games (The Games)
Les Jeux Olympiques (Les J.O.)
If you catch the Olympics on French TV, a couple of things jump out at you. They actually spend most of the time televising events instead of getting "up close and personal" with the guy's crippled mother or showing you how they make cheese from goat's milk in Kazakhstan. You'll also notice they have live coverage of lesser-known sports like kayaking *(le canoë kayak)* or fencing *(l'escrime)*—probably because those are the only sports in which France has a good chance to medal.

The Tour de France
Le Tour de France
The most famous bicycle race in the world takes place every year during the first three weeks in July and covers more than 1,800 miles. In recent decades, the success of Americans Greg LeMond (three-time winner) and record-holder Lance Armstrong (seven straight victories) has put cycling on the U.S. map. The reputation of the famed *maillot jaune* (the yellow jersey that the leader wears) has been severely damaged by recent doping scandals *(les*

scandales de dopage). These guys were more juiced up than José Canseco!

The Six Nations Tournament & the Rugby World Cup
Le Tournoi des Six Nations & La Coupe du Monde de Rugby
These are the two most prestigious international rugby competitions. The Six Nations is the oldest, and only France, England, Ireland, Italy, Scotland, and Wales compete. A rugby match is played in two halves, but the rugbymen are especially famous for the "third half" *(la troisième mi-temps)*: the heavy partying in bars that traditionally follows the game.

The French Open (Roland Garros)
Les Internationaux de France de Roland Garros
One of the four Grand Slam events in tennis, the French Open is played in Paris on clay in the spring. The arena is named after Roland Garros, an early French aviator who had nothing to do with tennis. But then again, the main Paris airport is named after Charles de Gaulle, a French president who had nothing to do with aviation.

The French Grand Prix & Le Mans
Le Grand Prix de France de Formule 1 & Les 24 heures du Mans
The Formula One French Grand Prix takes place every summer in Nevers Magny-Cours, 150 miles south of Paris, and features the fastest cars and best drivers in the world. At Le Mans, two drivers relay each other on the track for 24 hours straight. It was here in 1967 that a couple of Americans, Dan Gurney and A. J. Foyt, started the tradition of spraying Champagne after a race win. Although technically not held in France, the Monte Carlo Grand Prix on the French Riviera is another amazing race to watch because it takes place right in the middle of the city.

CHAPTER 9

HUNGRY FRENCH
LE FRANÇAIS AFFAMÉ

French cooking is no simple matter. Even *saying* "gastronomy" is hard. But unlike in the U.S. where lunch is a drive-through Happy Meal, in France people spend a lot of time in the kitchen and at the table. Here's a Tour de France of the best French grub talk.

·····Hunger
La faim

I'm starving.
J'ai la dalle.

I'm dying of hunger/of thirst.
Je crève *de faim/de soif.*

Let's get some…
Allons chercher de…

> **food**
> *la nourriture*

> **grub, eats**
> *la bouffe*

junk food
la malbouffe

fast food
la restauration rapide; le fast food

ethnic food
la bouffe exotique

Yum! That was...
Miam! C'était...

a good meal
un bon repas

really tasty
vraiment réussi

delicious
délicieux

scrumptious
un régal

filling
bien assez

I'm about to **bust a gut**.
*Je me suis **cassé le ventre**.*

I'm stuffed to the gills.
J'ai les dents du fond qui baignent.
Literally, "the food has backed up to my molars"

Yum-yum!
Miam miam!

It's really good!
C'est super bon!

Yuck!
Beurk!

Their food is crap.
Ils te font manger de la merde.

It's disgusting.
C'est dégueulasse.

I'm not gonna eat this...
Je vais pas bouffer...

bullshit
cette saloperie

garbage
cette pourriture

gooey thing
cette chose gluante

ungodly thing
cette chose immonde

steaming turd
cet étron fumant

·····At the restaurant
Au restaurant/Au restau

In France, even ordering water at a restaurant can be a trip through a minefield. Your waiter, possibly a smarmy, mustachioed dude who pretends not to understand your slight accent, will ask you to specify whether you want regular water (*l'eau*), mineral water (*l'eau minérale*), or mineral water without bubbles (*l'eau minérale plate*). Respond with equal disdain by saying, "Whatever's cheap and wet" (*Donnez-moi du liquide pas cher*). Then start pounding the table and chanting, "USA! USA! USA!" They love it when you do that.

FRENCH RESTAURANT CUSTOM AND ETIQUETTE)))

- The French eat late. Most restaurants open for dinner at 7:30 p.m.
- All-you-can-eat buffets are almost nonexistent in France. Why? Because the French would starve the entire family for two days, then show up and stuff their pockets.
- There's no bread plate; you put your bread directly on the table.
- You have to ask for the check or they won't bring it to you.

Bring me…
Apportez-moi…

> **the menu**
> *la carte*

> **bread**
> *du pain*

> **silverware**
> *des couverts*

> **the check**
> *l'addition*

Can we **order**?
*On peut **commander**?*

What do **you recommend**?
*Qu'est-ce que **vous recommandez**?*

Do I look like I wanna eat **frog legs**?
*J'ai une tête de mangeur de **cuisses de grenouilles**?*

Five bucks says you won't finish those **snails**.
*Je te parie cinq euros que tu termines pas **ces escargots**.*

HOW DO YOU WANT THAT COOKED?)))

POUR LA CUISSON?

In France, you can get your meat served either bleeding or burnt.
There's little in between. In fact, the French don't even have words for
medium or medium-rare. Most French opt for rare (a *lot* rarer than what
Americans go for), partly because French meat is so tender, thanks to
seasoned butchers who have mastered the technique of cutting with
the grain.

Very rare	*Bleu* (literally, "blue")
Rare	*Saignant* ("bleeding")
Medium well	*À point*
Well-done	*Bien cuit*
Burnt to a crisp	*Carbonisé*
I'm a vegetarian.	*Je suis végétarien(ne).*

What's taking so long? Did they have to head out **to the farm** to find my chicken, or what?
*Oh, mais c'est bien long! Ils sont allés le chercher **à la ferme** mon poulet, ou quoi?*

There's a fly in my soup. Call...
Il y a une mouche dans ma soupe. Appelez-moi...

> **the manager**
> *le patron*

> **the chef**
> *le chef*

> **the cook**
> *le cuistot*

> **the waiter/the waitress**
> *le serveur/la serveuse*

> **the wine steward**
> *le sommelier*

I don't have any dough on me, but I could **do the dishes** to settle up.
*J'ai pas d'argent mais je peux **faire la vaisselle** pour régler la note.*

·····French Cuisine
La cuisine française

The same way that a hamburger with fries is the ultimate American dish, the *steak frites* (steak with fries) is the ole standby in France. Yet to the French, fries are considered Belgian. In fact, it's common to hear Belgians called "fry eaters" (*mangeurs de frites*). In addition to this national dish, France has a variety of regional specialties:

THE NORTHWEST

> **Yo, can I get some...?**
> *Ho, je peux avoir...?*

les moules frites
A big bowl of steaming, fragrant mussels accompanied by piping-hot fries

la coquille Saint-Jacques
Scallops cooked in butter with onions and shallots, topped with grated cheese

la tarte Tatin
The French version of apple pie, served upside down and caramelized

les bêtises de Cambrai
Delicious mint candies

les macarons
Miniature cakes made with almonds and frosting

la crème Chantilly
Whipped cream with a fancy name

les crêpes
Crepes; you can have them for lunch, topped with cheese, ham, and eggs, or as dessert, covered in chocolate, Nutella, sugar, or jam.

THE EAST

You gotta try the…
Tu devrais essayer…

la choucroute
In the Alsace-Lorraine region, a big plate of sauerkraut comes with hot dogs (saucisses de Francfort), a slice of ham (*jambon*), and steamed potatoes.

l'andouillette
Chitlins, or, for those of you not from the South, pig intestines; fittingly, andouille is also slang for "dumbass"

le boudin
Blood sausage
Also slang for a very ugly person

la quiche lorraine
There are different kinds; the famous Lorraine quiche is ham and cheese.

le bœuf bourguignon
A classic French stew of
cubed beef slow-cooked in
red wine and broth

la fondue bourguignonne
A beef fondue in which
tender, thin-sliced beef
is cooked in butter and
oil and dipped in flavorful
sauces

les escargots de Bourgogne
A French delicacy:
cooked snails slurped
down with lots of butter and
parsley—dee-lish

PROVENCE AND RIVIERA

This place makes a mean...
Ici ils font...

une super salade niçoise
A classic salad served with fresh veggies, boiled egg,
tuna, anchovies, and olive oil

une succulente bouillabaisse
Like a French gumbo, with fish, potatoes, and soup

de la très bonne daube provençale
Red wine–marinated beef, cut in strips and served
with pasta

de bons calissons
Candied almonds sweetened with crystallized
cantaloupe

CORSICA

Don't leave without tasting the...
Ne partez pas sans avoir goûté...

le figatelli
Pork-liver sausage served hot and dripping with
delicious fat and garlic

le fromage corse
Incredibly stinky Corsican cheese made from goat's and sheep's milk

SOUTHWEST

What! You've never had...?
Quoi! tu n'as jamais mangé de...?

Roquefort
A strong blue cheese

cassoulet
A perfect winter dish made with duck, sausage, goose fat, and beans; sop up the drippings with crusty bread

THE ALPS

I'm gonna go into a food coma if I eat any more...
Je vais tomber dans le coma si je reprends encore...

de la fondue savoyarde
Cheese fondue; traditional dish, originally from Switzerland—you dip small pieces of bread into a crock with thick melted Swiss cheese (*fondre* means "to melt"); great after skiing

du gratin dauphinois
Gratin-style potatoes with sour cream and oven-melted cheese

•••••Cuttin' the cheese
Tranches de fromage

France has more varieties of cheese than any other country. Much like wine, every region in France has its own type. They come in all shapes, forms, colors, and smells, from the neutral, don't-offend-anybody kinds to those that smell worse than sweaty animals having sex in a barnyard. Cheese is such a part of the national identity that the French fold it into everyday sayings, like *N'en fais pas tout un fromage* (literally, don't turn it into cheese), which is how they say "Don't get your panties in a wad."

Pass the...
Passe-moi...

Cut me some...
Coupe-moi un morceau de...

Damn, that...smells funky.
Putain, ce....sent putain de drôle.

> *le brie:* A mild, creamy and universally popular cow's milk cheese

> *le camembert:* Also from cow's milk and relatively mild

> *le gruyère:* Basically Swiss cheese, only way better than that crap you're used to getting from the "sandwich artists" at Subway; it's made from goat's milk, is dense and sharp, and comes in small servings

> *le Bleu d'Auvergne:* From the center region of France called Auvergne, a smoother type of blue cheese

> *le Saint-Nectaire:* Another classic from Auvergne; the most commonly produced farmer cheese in France

la mimolette: Made in the north of France near the Belgian border; cow's milk cheese whose taste and orange color make it similar to our cheddars

le boursin: Famous soft cheese from Normandy, with a pepper touch, that reached stardom with a successful worldwide TV campaign that went, "*Du pain, du vin, du Boursin*" (bread, wine, Boursin!)

la tomme de chèvre: As the name indicates, a goat milk cheese from the Savoie region: small, rounded, hard, and tasty

Are those **worms** in that cheese?
*C'est **des vers** là dans ce fromage?*

That cheese **stinks** like dirty socks!
*Il **sent** trop les pieds ce fromage!*

Damn, that cheese is **seriously nasty**!
*Putain comme **il shlingue** ce fromage!*

•••••The ABC's of sandwiches
Le B-A BA du sandwich

Except for the Bagnat and the Club, which come on hamburger buns and sliced bread, all French sandwiches are made with baguettes. While there are places called *sandwicheries* (can you guess what they serve?), you can get a sandwich almost anywhere food is sold.

I'd kill for a...
Je tuerais pour un...

croque-monsieur
The king of French sandwiches. It's basically just a grilled ham and cheese sandwich, but you have to eat it with a fork because the whole thing comes smothered in melted Gruyère cheese.

croque-madame
Same as above, but with a fried egg

pan bagnat
A deliciously slimy, stinky concoction of anchovies, tomatoes, black olives, olive oil, and onions served on a hamburger bun

parisien
Ham, lettuce, butter: the original version of Parisian "fast food"

merguez frites
This spicy lamb sandwich stuffed with fries is the classic three-in-the-morning, drunk-and-still-partyin'-hard, fast food meal-of-choice for most French. It's also the sporting event equivalent of the American ballpark hot dog. Watch out for the harissa sauce on the merguez—it'll light your ass on fire!

Hey! **Easy on the** *harissa*!
*Oh! **Doucement avec la** harissa!*

I'd give my own life for a **hot dog**.
*Je donnerais ma vie pour un **hot-dog**.*
Never translate "hot-dog" literally *(un chien chaud)*, or the counter guy will either look at you as if you just crapped on his floor or will serve you somebody's pet.

This is one **dry, boring-ass sandwich**.
*Celui-ci est un vrai **sandwich au pain**.*
If your sandwich is too dry and there's not much of anything in it, you just call that shit a "bread sandwich."

COFFEE CULTURE)))

An espresso	*Un express*
A double espresso	*Un double*
An espresso with a drop of cream	*Une noisette*
Coffee diluted with extra water	*Un café allongé; un café américain*
An American coffee with milk	*Un café au lait*

Every time I drink coffee, it makes me want to take a shit.
A chaque fois que je bois du café, ça me donne envie de chier.

·····Food spots
Points bouffe

The famous Michelin guides provide reviews on all the best restaurants in France. The French take these ratings seriously: One chef famously committed suicide after his restaurant was stripped of a star. For a top restaurant like Paris's Tour d'Argent, you'll have to reserve weeks or months in advance and be prepared to shell out some serious cash. Those of us with humbler tastes and shallower pockets have cheaper alternatives.

Mickey D's
MacDo
Pulp Fiction stole our thunder and already taught you that French McDonald's serve beer, and that a quarter-pounder is called a *royale with cheese*. But it didn't teach you that French farmers, none too happy about processed meat, hate Mickey D's so much that every once in a while they try to bulldoze them. They even bombed a McDonald's in Millau, France's equivalent of the Midwest!

You wanna hit Mickey D's tonight?
On se fait *un MacDo ce soir?*

To **get some grub** or to ***bomb it***?
*Pour **aller chercher à bouffer** ou pour **le faire sauter**?*

Quick
The French fast food competitor to McDonald's. French fast food restaurants *do not* have automatic refills on drinks. (It'd kinda be a problem with the beer.)

Brasseries Chez Clément
Good for traditional French meals and wine.

Pizza Païl/Pizza del Arte
Most French pizza comes thin à la New York Style. In the south of France, you'll find pizza trucks (*camion pizza*) that cruise through the neighborhood during the week or when there are major sporting events. They actually have wood-burning ovens and make it fresh.

Bistro Romain
A decent Italian chain known for its all-you-can-eat appetizers, a rarity by French standards. Kind of like Olive Garden's all-you-can-eat breadsticks, but way awesomer. See how much smoked salmon carpaccio you can eat before hurling.

Buffalo Grill
A bad pun on "Buffalo Bill." Vegetarians and people who can't stand kids should sit it out in the car.

La Cafétéria (Flunch, Casino)
Cafeterias in France are self-service restaurants. Picture those American chains like Denny's that cater to the blue-hair crowd, and you're on the right track. Proof that the French *can* prepare bad food. Grab your tray and go…somewhere else?

La Taverne de Maître Kanter
A brasserie-style chain specializing in sauerkraut and beer. Mmmm…sauerkraut and beer.

Léon de Bruxelles
The *moules frites* (mussels and fries) specialists. Dip your fries in the mussel juice at the bottom of the bowl for a bit of gustatory heaven.

La Brioche Dorée
A good pastry chain to snag breakfast or lunch on the fly (they also serve salads and sandwiches). Try their *tartelette aux framboises* (raspberry tart) or a slice of their flan. You won't go wrong.

·····Other Ulysses Press Titles

Dirty Chinese: Everyday Slang from "What's Up?" to "F*%# Off!"
MATT COLEMAN & EDMUND BACKHOUSE, **$10.00**

Dirty Chinese includes phrases for every situation, even expressions to convince a local official that you have waited long enough and tipped him plenty already. A pronunciation guide, a reference dictionary and sample dialogues make this guide invaluable for those traveling to China.

Dirty German: Everyday Slang from "What's Up?" to "F*%# Off!"
DANIEL CHAFFEY, **$10.00**

Dirty German provides enough insults and swear words to offend every person in Germany—without even mentioning that the Japanese make better cars —as well as explicit sex terms that'll even embarrass the women of Hamburg's infamous red light district.

Dirty Spanish: Everyday Slang from "What's Up?" to "F*%# Off!"
JUAN CABALLERO & NICK DENTON-BROWN, **$10.00**

This handbook features slang for both Spain and Latin America. It includes a section on native banter that will help readers make friends over a pitcher of sangría and convince the local taco maker that it's OK to spice things up with a few fresh habaneros.

Dirty Italian: Everyday Slang
from "What's Up?" to "F*%# Off!"
GABRIELLE EUVINO, **$10.00**

Nobody speaks in strictly formal address anymore. Certainly not in Italy, where the common expression shouted on the streets is far from textbook Italian. This book fills in the gap between how people really talk in Italy and what Italian language students are taught.

Dirty Japanese: Everyday Slang
from "What's Up?" to "F*%# Off!"
MATT FARGO, **$10.00**

Even in traditionally minded Japan, slang from its edgy pop culture constantly enter into common usage. This book fills in the gap between how people really talk in Japan and what Japanese language students are taught.

Dirty Russian: Everyday Slang
from "What's Up?" to "F*%# Off!"
ADRIEN CLAUTRIER & HENRY ROWE, **$10.00**

Nothing is censored in *Dirty Russian*. An invaluable guide for off-the-beaten-path travelers going to Russia, this book is packed with enough insults and swear words to offend every person in Russia without even mentioning that they lost the Cold War.

To order these books call 800-377-2542 or 510-601-8301, fax 510-601-8307, e-mail ulysses@ulyssespress.com, or write to Ulysses Press, P.O. Box 3440, Berkeley, CA 94703. All retail orders are shipped free of charge. California residents must include sales tax. Allow two to three weeks for delivery.

·····About the Authors

Adrien Clautrier is a self-employed mechanic born and raised in Marseille, France. A motorcycle and automobile enthusiast, he has completed two US coast-to-coast trips, one on a Harley Davidson and the other in a Cadillac. When he is not in his garage or on the road, he reads non-stop (especially Frédéric Dard's *San Antonio* series) or listens to the stand-up comedies of the late French comedian Coluche.

Henry Rowe left Berkeley to play soccer in France. He never made it out of the amateur ranks, but stayed for the used bookstores and St-Émilion wine cellars. He currently lives in Ménilmontant in Paris, frequents Mon Chien Stupide, and listens to everything from Serge Gainsbourg to Toulouse's Jerry Spider Gang.